Crappit Heids for Tea

Crappit Heids for Tea

Recollections of Highland Childhood

— ◆ —

Iby Fraser and Ann Gray

Introduction by Dr Anne-Marie Tindley
Compiled by Chris Fletcher

BIRLINN

First published in 2012 by
Birlinn Limited
West Newington House
10 Newington Road
Edinburgh
EH9 1QS

www.birlinn.co.uk

ISBN: 978 1 78027 082 1

British Library Cataloguing-in-Publication Data
A catalogue record for this book is available from the British Library

Typeset by Iolaire Typesetting, Newtonmore
Printed and bound by Clays Ltd, St Ives plc

Contents

———— ✦ ————

List of Illustrations	vii
Acknowledgments	ix
Foreword by Alistair, Lord Strathnaver	xi
Map	xiii

1. Shinness Estate: the Reclamations and Sutherland Shooting Lodges, 1850–1920   1
   by Dr Anne-Marie Tindley

2. Iby Fraser and Her Family, Shinness and Lairg   17

3. Recollections of Highland Childhood   21
   by Iby Fraser

4. Ann Gray, of Colaboll, Lairg   81

5. Changed Days in the Colaboll Steading   87
   by Ann Gray

List of Plates

———— ◆ ————

Iby Fraser's manuscript, 'A Wisp of History'.

Reclamation works at Colaboll in the 1870s.

Reclamation works etching from Dunrobin Castle.

Monument to Kenneth Murray of Geanies as it is today.

The Duke's luncheon house on the bank of Loch Shin as it is today.

Daisy and Iby Fraser and Feannach the dog.

John and Margaret Fraser, Daisy and Iby at the Keeper's House, Shinness Lodge, c. 1908.

John Fraser, Iby's father.

Margaret Fraser, Iby's mother.

Iby Fraser

Uncle Donald, Normanna, Daisy, Iby and Bob Munro.

The coming of the car – at the Sutherland Arms Hotel Lairg, c. 1911.

J. R. Campbell's car.

Taking home the peats, with Ben More Assynt in the background.

Tinkers' encampment near loch Shin.

Tinkers on the road in the 1930s.

Shooting party at Shinness on the Aird in the 1920s.

Looking west towards Shinness Farm (now West Shinness Lodge) from the Aird in the 1920s, on ground now flooded.

Shooting party on Cnoc an Ulbhaidh, Shinness.

A page from M.E. Sanderson's game book, noting MES and Fraser as guns.

House party at Shinness Lodge in the 1920s.

Coláboll Farm before the First World War, with Alec Gray as a boy, on the left

Some of the Gray family, probably in the mid 1930s.

Graduation portrait of Ann Gray.

Ann Gray.

Acknowledgements

———— ◆ ————

Many people have enthusiastically helped me to compile this book. First, thanks to the SWRI in Lairg who, many years ago, had the idea of encouraging Iby Fraser and Ann Gray to present their recollections. Both of them wrote these down so we can read them ourselves. Iby's recollections were addressed to my mother Margaret Fletcher, who lived at Shinness Lodge from 1958 until 2007. Iby suggested that they be burned once read, and I must therefore thank my mother (a magpie collector in the book world) for not doing so.

There are then many other people to mention.

Dr Anne-Marie Tindley of Glasgow Caledonian University has written the historical introduction and also found in Reading the photographs of the steam ploughs doing their work in the 1870s at Shinness. She diligently spent many hours to research Shinness. Her knowledge of the history of Sutherland has been a wonderful source for the book.

Robin Johnston (Iby's great nephew and former pupil) and Paul Gray (Ann Gray's cousin) have given much help in providing additional material, biographies and photographs which have found their way into the book.

In addition, Annette Parrott (whose grandfather Reginald Maudsley purchased West Shinness), Pete Campbell (whose great grandfather was J.R. Campbell) and Angela Sutherland (Charlie Armstrong's grand-daughter) have provided photographs, and Lord Strathnaver has supported the project and enabled us to use the image of the reclamations which hangs at Dunrobin Castle.

The Lairg Historical Society chaired by Rev. John Leslie Goskirk were early supporters of the project, and John held a reading of the book when it was first typed up.

The publishing team needs special mention – Andrew Simmons at Birlinn, and the editors who helped to refine the text, Karen Howlett and Deborah Warner, put a lot of effort into making the book readable.

Thanks to all of them and the many others who have read the text and had a hand in the final production. I hope the result is as much fun to read as it has been to compile.

Chris Fletcher
Shinness Lodge
May 2012
www.shinnesslodge.co.uk

Foreword

———— ✦ ————

Scotland is often described as Europe's last wilderness, but as the history of this part of the Highlands shows, many people lived there and attempts have been made to improve the living from the wild moorlands for a long time.

By the time Iby Fraser and Ann Gray were born at Shinness, sheep and cattle grazing was only part of the land use; fishing, shooting and stalking were an important addition. Iby describes far more than the life of the gamekeeper working for tenants who took long leases of the lodge. Her lively story is of a happy childhood in a family deeply embedded in the rural Highland life where each member had a part to play. Ann's story of the first 100 years of her family on the farm at Colaboll describes the people she met and the life of the farm. When roads and communications were poor, rural neighbours depended on each other, and the Fraser and Gray families were an important part of the local community.

These accounts are a chance to discover what day to day life was like then, far from the cities. They open a small window onto the benefits and the hardships of Highland gamekeeping and farming in the early 1900s, a time when attempts were being made by the Sutherland family to create better economic use of the land, bringing more people and prosperity to the Highlands.

Over the sixty years since the Second World War, there have been huge changes in the Highlands. Tree planting, power supply, renewable energy, vastly improved communications and tourism have developed land use beyond farming and sport. No longer does a small number of wealthy visitors stay in some style for months at a time as was the case when these memoirs were written. Today many more people can enjoy landscape, nature and the hills during shorter holidays at the places like Shinness and other Highland houses. Visitors find a landscape where much of the land with its sheep, birds and deer, lodges and castles looks little different in their moor and mountain settings described here. But the way of life described by Iby and Ann and their families has vanished. *Crappit Heids for Tea* brings back a harder and simpler way of life but also captures its warmth and comfortable certainties.

I hope that reading Iby's and Ann's memoirs will spark your interest.

Alistair, Lord Strathnaver
Dunrobin Castle
May 2012

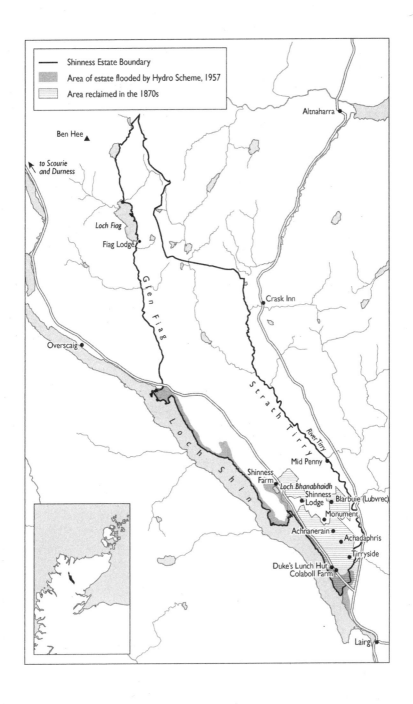

Shinness Estate Boundary

Area of estate flooded by Hydro Scheme, 1957

Area reclaimed in the 1870s

Altnaharra

Ben Hee

to Scourie
and Durness

Loch Fiag

Fiag Lodge

Glen Fiag

Crask Inn

Overscaig

Strath Tirry

River Tirry

Loch Shin

Mid Penny

Shinness
Farm

Loch Bhanabhaidh

Shinness
Lodge

Blarbuie (Lubvrec)

Monument

Achnanerain

Achadaphris

Tirryside

Duke's Lunch Hut
Colaboll Farm

Lairg

Shinness Estate: the Reclamations and Sutherland Shooting Lodges, 1850–1920

---- ◆ ----

Introduction

This book is set in and around Shinness, near Lairg, in central Sutherland, an area that has witnessed human settlement from the earliest times, although Iby Fraser's and Ann Gray's stories deal mainly with the early twentieth century onwards. By that time, the land around Shinness and Lairg had for centuries been in the hands of the earls of Sutherland. The first earl was William de Moravia, with the title dating from around 1230. He was descended from a Flemish nobleman, Freskin, who settled at Duffus in Morayshire in the mid-twelfth century. At around the same time, other Flemish immigrant artisans were encouraged by King David I to start the weaving trade and settle in villages. A long line of earls, based at Dunrobin Castle near Golspie, descended from that time, occasionally through daughters who inherited the title. One of these, in the late eighteenth century, was Elizabeth Gordon, the 19th countess, who married Lord (later Marquis of) Stafford, who also became

1

the first Duke of Sutherland. By that time, life spent accumulating cattle and skirmishing with neighbouring clans such as the Mackays had given way to a money-based economy in which landowners sought to increase their cash returns. This change was strongly promoted following the 1745 Jacobite Rising, as the government required clan chiefs to be in London (where money was needed) in order to reduce the chances of further unrest.

From the 1790s, the population in Lairg parish, and of Sutherland (and indeed of Britain as a whole) had been steadily increasing and did not reduce until the early twentieth century. With more efficient agriculture, better public health and improved food supplies, Sutherland's population continued to grow until it reached a peak of around 26,000 as recorded in the 1861 census.[1] Real population decline occurred in Sutherland in the interwar years after 1918, when, at its lowest, the population for the county hovered at around 11,000.[2] The population varied seasonally: many moved to follow the fishing industry in the summer, while being at home to cultivate crofts in spring, and many more would have worked as casual labour on the new sheep farms created in the nineteenth century.

The Sutherland Estate was, by the mid-nineteenth century, the largest landed estate in western Europe. Owning over one million acres, the earls (dukes from 1833) of Sutherland were the largest of Britain's private landowners, while most of their wealth came from the Stafford connection. As earls, following the purchase of Mackay lands in 1829, they owned almost the whole county of Sutherland, granting them

---

1. *Census of Scotland*, 1911 (Edinburgh, 1912), p. 2233.
2. *Census of Scotland*, 1921 (Edinburgh, 1923), p. 1874.

control over land occupied by a large population, the bulk of which were small tenants or crofters. This control over wide acres led to a uniform approach to estate policy, including building works and design, a fact that is strikingly apparent in the appearance of the Sutherland shooting lodges. It also led to the ability to undertake large-scale economic and social restructuring on the estate from the early to late nineteenth century.

Sheep farming

In the very early nineteenth century, the estate owners, Lord Stafford and his wife, the Countess of Sutherland, and their estate managers, principally William Young and later James Loch, attempted to re-model the estate along more economic lines.

They created great sheep farms covering perhaps half of the total area of the estate, moving the small tenants and crofters out of this land, events which took place in the Lairg and Shinness area between 1807 and 1821. Experienced shepherds, who knew the ways of Cheviot sheep, were recruited from the Scottish Borders. The estate invested especially in the interior pastures of the county and for some decades the money spent to develop these farms was repaid in increased rents.[3] The sheep-farming tenants, who came from all over Britain, particularly the north of England, also prospered and many of them made fortunes in the middle decades of the nineteenth century. This prosperity came under attack by the 1860s as a result of falling sheep and

---

3. E. Richards, *Debating the Highland Clearances* (Edinburgh, 2007), pp. 3–11.

cattle prices due to new supplies coming from such countries as New Zealand, Australia and Argentina and, from the 1870s, general agricultural depression.[4] Ironically, it was in the early 1860s that the population of the county peaked. A vast sum had been invested in sheep farms and the economic downturn in that sector required the estate to diversify its sources of income.

Sportings

Luckily, the vogue for game fishing, shooting and stalking (known as 'sporting') was starting to take hold in the Highlands, led by royal approval at Balmoral and emulated across the region. The Sutherland Estate began a long process of conversion from sheep farms to sporting leases, in some cases adding sporting capability to existing farms. This began in the eastern and central areas of the county in the 1850s (Loch Choire, Ben Armine and along the Helmsdale River, for example), spreading to the west (the Reay Forest and Glencanisp, for instance) by the early 1890s.[5] By the time of the great Sutherland land sales between 1916 and 1920, huge portions of the estate had been turned over to sportings and the income from these tenancies dominated the rental rolls in much the same way as that from sheep farms had decades before.

Although the rewards of this conversion in the form of a healthy rental roll were obvious, sporting tenancies required

4. W. Orr, *Deer Forests, Landlords and Crofters: The Western Highlands in Victorian and Edwardian Times* (Edinburgh, 1982), pp. 16–22.
5. Ibid., pp. 31–6; A. Tindley, *The Sutherland Estate: Estate Management, Aristocratic Decline and Land Reform* (Edinburgh, 2010), pp. 110–12.

a good deal of capital investment by the estate, especially in the initial stages. New boundaries had to be mapped out, strict rules regarding muir (heather) burning and annual 'bags' were set and, of course, suitable lodges had to be built for the tenants.[6] Investment along these lines by the Sutherland Estate was vast. No fewer than 26 dedicated sporting estates were set up, all requiring investment and management. In addition, 32 farms were developed for sportings. In return, the estate received reliable rents from their new tenants; by 1897, just under 50 per cent of the total rental roll came from the sporting tenancies and, unlike crofting and farming rents, there were never any arrears.[7]

Sporting estates and tenancies became well established in Scotland, particularly in the Highlands, where they often came to be a significant part of economic life in the region.[8] Central to the landscape are the shooting lodges of the Highlands; often grand architectural affairs which dominated the scenery, expressing the economic and social importance of the business of sport, and of their owners and tenants. The shooting estates were important to the local economy in the north of Scotland, providing casual employment to many during the 'season'. Iby Fraser recalls that Shinness Estate employed no fewer than 20 ghillies to look after its 25,000 acres in the early twentieth century, for example. The Sutherland Arms Hotel at Lairg employed seventeen ghillies in the inter-war years for the trout and salmon fishing. This seasonal existence cannot have been easy. Iby remembers one ghillie being asked by a guest, 'How's the world treating you,

---

6. See the extensive correspondence in National Library of Scotland [hereafter NLS], Acc. 10225, Shootings and Games, for example.

7. NLS, Acc. 10225, Rentals, Abstract for Dunrobin (1897).

8. W. Orr, op. cit., pp. 33–7.

nowadays, Hughie?' His answer came back: 'Well, in truth, not very often!'

Most Highland estates developed the sporting potential of their lands in the nineteenth century, but perhaps no other estate with such enthusiasm and commitment of capital expenditure as the Sutherland Estate. More famous for its development of sheep farming in the early nineteenth century, the estate made over huge tracts of territory to sport from the 1850s up to the 1890s. They let it in long-term tenancies, complete with lodges, to rich tenants seeking to join the fashion for shooting, stalking and fishing, much enjoyed by wealthy industrialists and City men as well as the aristocracy.[9] This was facilitated by the growth of the railways in the middle decades of the nineteenth century, which in Sutherland was financed almost entirely by the 3rd duke, in particular the line from Inverness to Wick and Thurso.[10]

One of the requirements of the development of sporting estates in the region was the building of lodges for the new sporting owners and tenants. These were large-scale building projects in some of the most remote places of the British Isles; building in such challenging circumstances required large sums in expenditure on design, materials and labour. Hope Lodge, on the north coast of Sutherland, for example, was then accessible only from the sea; it was decided that stone was too difficult a building material to transport there, so the lodge was designed and built only from wood, with both walls and roof protected by slate.[11] Lodges were also unusual

---

9. A. Tindley, *The Sutherland Estate, 1850–1920* (Edinburgh, 2010), pp. 110–12.

10. NLS, Acc. 10225, Sutherland Estates Papers, Railways.

11. NLS, Acc. 10225, Architect's correspondence, 256, William Fowler to John Crawford, 20 Jan. 1882; 258, William Fowler to John Crawford, 30 Aug. 1883.

in their levels of design and comfort; gas, then electric lighting, bathrooms and toilets were all at the forefront of the design, to enable rich tenants used to metropolitan luxury to shoot, stalk and fish in their accustomed comfort. Additionally, lodges had to have accommodation for house-keepers, cooks and other servants; cottages for dedicated gamekeepers; kennels and stables for their dogs and ponies; and larders for the deer, fish and birds that were bagged. All of this was a large investment for estates to make, but the rewards were proportionate: until well into the twentieth century rentals from sport propped up many estate incomes while they were battered from other directions as a result of falling sheep and cattle prices, and from the 1870s general agricultural depression.[12]

The development of the sporting estates in Sutherland follows the general pattern of most Highland estates, except for the large scale of the enterprise there; Shinness Estate had, however, some unique features in its history.

Shinness Lodge and the Sutherland Reclamations

In 1861, the 3rd Duke of Sutherland inherited his estate from his father. He was keen to invest in it and to further his personal interest in the latest agricultural steam technology. In 1869, he began a series of land reclamations in Sutherland, with the intention of converting unproductive low-lying moorland into productive arable acres.[13] This was a huge project, requiring hundreds of men to labour on it; indeed, the reclamations were an important source of casual labour

12. A. Tindley, *The Sutherland Estate, 1850–1920* (Edinburgh, 2010), p. 5.
13. Ibid., p. 34.

for Sutherland men in the 1870s and early 1880s. The land was marked out, then drained and fenced, and ploughed with the latest steam plough sets from John Fowler and Company. The duke, a noted enthusiast for steam power, first saw Fowler's engines and ploughs at work in Egypt in the 1860s and was inspired to use them on his own land, far to the north.[14] The land was then expected to be leased, with new buildings, to sheep farmers, who would be able to grow oats as food for farm workers and as fodder crops for their flocks. As sheep numbers had grown, the arable land available to grow winter forage crops became insufficient in Sutherland. In order to feed them in the winter, sheep needed to make an annual pilgrimage into Caithness, or fodder had to be imported.[15] The main purpose of the land reclamations was to grow the extra fodder required 'at home'.

These land reclamations took place at Kinbrace, in the strath of Kildonan, Clashmore in Assynt, Ribigill near Tongue and, most importantly, at Shinness near Lairg. The Shinness reclamations were the first and therefore the 'flagship' of the duke's reclamation projects; they also saw the largest sum of money expended on them – no less than £184,454 – most of which went on wages and new buildings although, at £1,000 per set, the steam ploughs were not cheap either.[16]

Iby notes:

In the beginning of the nineteenth century the Parish of Lairg was entirely moorland with the exception of areas of land reclaimed by hand trenching. The only crops were

14. H. Bonnett, *The Saga of the Steam Plough* (Newton Abbott, 1965), p. 54.

15. A. Tindley, *The Sutherland Estate, 1850–1920* (Edinburgh, 2010), p. 34.

16. Ibid., pp. 35, 38.

potatoes and oats. With the introduction of Cheviot sheep from the south, the older breeds of Kerry and Blackface sheep were driven out. The hill land was admirably adapted to this new breed and was then let to sheep farmers from Northumberland.

About 1870, the Duke of Sutherland, who owned the land, was very concerned about the large amount of food for man and animal that had to be imported. He called in Mr Kenneth Murray of Geanies, Ross-shire, a gentleman of vast agricultural experience, to make a survey of the Shinness valley, with a view to increasing its arable area in order to raise the sufficiency of oatmeal for the inhabitants and winter food for the animals.

From this beginning developed what was to become one of the largest and most notable agricultural operations of its kind in the United Kingdom. Altogether six farms were reclaimed, namely Dalchork, Achfrish, Achnairn, Colaboll, Lubvrec and West Shinness, ranging from 200 to 475 acres arable, and amounting to 2,000 acres in all. The work was personally supervised by the duke, and it had so wide a reputation that it attracted many eminent visitors, including the Prince of Wales in 1876, who inspected the work minutely. The whole Shinness valley was a scene of intense activity, with no fewer than 14 steam engines at work, while several hundred men were busily engaged in drainage, ploughing, clearing stones, erecting dykes, making roads and building houses and steadings.

One man recalls how his grandfather used to tell of his experiences in those days. He would, with several others, set off as soon as Monday morning came to walk as much as 20 miles to the reclamation area, taking with him his week's rations – half a stone of oatmeal and a bottle of treacle. The whole operation made a considerable impact on the life of the parish and could not have failed to impress visitors as marvellous.

In conjunction with the reclamations, the duke opened limestone quarries at the Aird on the north bank of Loch Shin. Here he had lime kilns built, where the limestone was burnt and would then improve the fertility of the newly reclaimed land. A steamer was launched on Loch Shin to tow the barges laden with limestone to Lairg, where lime kilns were also built at the station. Lime was sent to all parts of the county where the duke's other schemes of reclamation were being continued.

On Cokaboll Farm, overlooking Loch Shin, there is a little wooden bungalow that is still known as the 'Luncheon House'. During the reclamation period, it was built for the duke. He had lunch there when he came to visit the 'works' then going on. Having travelled on his own railway, in his own train, from Golspie, and having sailed from Lairg in his steam launch, he was met below the Luncheon House by his coach, drawn by a pair of spanking greys.

The 3rd Duke was, as Iby notes, guided in his reclamation programme by Mr Kenneth Murray of Geanies, a noted agriculturalist of northern Scotland and a keen proponent of the wonders of steam power. He and the duke became good friends and when he died rather suddenly midway through the works, the duke erected a monument to Murray's memory at Achnairn on Shinness. Recently restored, it has a good view of the main reclamations and can still be visited.

By the early 1880s, the land reclamations had been on-going for 11 years. It was becoming starkly apparent that the land would not be as productive, and neither were the farms to be as economically successful, as the duke and his estate management had hoped. The bottom had fallen out of the sheep market in the late 1870s and there were no prospective tenants for the new farms around Shinness and Lairg.[17] The estate was forced to keep these new farms, created out of the bog at vast cost, in hand, while advertising them for rent again and again in the agricultural press. By the time of the visit of the Royal Commission on conditions for the crofters of the Highlands in 1883, the Sutherland Estate factors were openly labelling the reclamations a failure, economically and agriculturally.[18]

The Sutherland Estate needed to find a new use for the land around Shinness and, given the wider demand for sporting tenancies and their more certain economic success, Shinness Lodge was built towards the end of the reclamation project, between 1882 and 1885. Compared to most of the many lodges built by the Sutherland Estate, it is relatively modest. Constructed in granite, the house now accommodates six couples (following conversion of a bedroom to a bathroom in its early years) with attic bedrooms for female staff. The male seasonal staff were housed in a bothy by the Keeper's House at the foot of the drive. Mrs Fleming, wife of John Fraser's successor as keeper, Alec Fleming, recalled the fun the staff had in the summer evenings during the 1920s and 1930s, amusing themselves at the bothy with ceilidhs and dancing, while Mrs Fleming played the 'squeezebox', a button-based accordion.

The first tenant of Shinness, a Mr Michael Edwin Sanderson, of Wakefield, took his lease in 1882 before the new lodge

17. A. Tindley, op. cit., pp. 45–7.
18. Parliamentary Papers [PP] 1884 XXXIII–XXXVI, *Evidence and Report of the Commissioners of Inquiry into the Condition of the Crofters and Cottars in the Highlands and Island of Scotland* [hereafter *Napier Commission Evidence*], pp. 1642, 2526.

had been started.[19] The estate quickly mobilised, however, and work began that year, taking until 1885 for final completion at a total cost of £2169.2s.4d.[20] The estate did not bear the burden of this cost alone, however; Mr Sanderson paid £642 per year in rent and agreed to pay 7 per cent interest on the first £400 and then 5 per cent interest on the remaining balance of the building costs, a financial arrangement that had been in place for most building works associated with the reclamations, and certainly one which ameliorated the duke's risk to some extent.[21] He also invested over the years in sporting, seeding Loch Fiag with 10,000 rainbow trout in 1907. These fish are famous escapees and anglers often claimed they had caught 'sea-trout' in northern Loch Shin in the following years. The duke still had to furnish the lodge for his tenant, which set him back a further £200, and create the 'approach' or driveway, for a further £79, but this had all been completed by 1885, and aside from some repairs and later improvements (a WC toilet was installed in 1906), he could expect healthy returns on this investment.[22]

The estate was less successful in finding a tenant for Shinness Farm but eventually did so, firstly in Mr John Blake (1883–89) and then in Mr John R. Campbell, in 1889.[23]

19. This gave Sanderson the opportunity to influence the design and finishing of the lodge; see NLS, Acc. 10225, Architect's correspondence, 257, William Fowler to Edwin Sanderson, 28 Aug. 1882; 6 Sept. 1882; 4 Dec. 1882; 24 Jan. 1883; 7 Mar. 1883.
20. NLS, Acc. 10225, Shootings and Game, Shinness.
21. NLS, Acc. 10853, Register of Demands, F, p. 320.
22. NLS, Acc. 10853, Register of Demands, G, pp. 65, 152; Specifications, 562.
23. NLS, Acc. 10225, Reclamations, 41, 'Shinness farm: Memorandum of conditions for lease of Shinness arable and sheep farm by the Duke of Sutherland,' 2 Jan. 1878; Acc. 10225, Farms, 41, 'Valuation of stock', 31 Dec. 1883, signed by John Blake and J.R. Campbell; 'Memorandum of conditions of let of Shinness farm to M.E. Sanderson and J.R. Campbell', 5 Oct. 1889.

Campbell had in fact supervised some of the reclamation work at Shinness, and managed the farm before taking the leap to tenancy of the new farm and, despite its troubled start, made a success of the venture.[24] Iby recalls one of the Shinness shepherds, Charlie Armstrong, who was a grandson of a Borders shepherd recruited in the early 1800s, telling her in the 1970s (when he was the 'oldest inhabitant') of starting work with 'JRC' at the turn of the century:

His most vivid memories were paying for his schooling – 3s 6d a month and also paying for his school books; the lack of variety in the food – porridge, potatoes, herring and the only bread, oatcakes; how the *People's Journal* and the *Inverness Chronicle* were read from cover to cover and handed round as precious as gold; how the whole community went into mourning if one member died; and how every house kept an open door; how dances and ceilidhs helped to pass the long winter months; how his first wage was 1s 3d per day, but withheld if he was off ill or unable to work because of bad weather.

Campbell died in 1933, a respected local figure who had done well out of farming, despite the troubling wider economic context for sheep farming over the decades when he was tenant. He was helped, initially at least, by his neighbour, Mr Sanderson, who, as well as being the shooting tenant of Shinness Lodge, became involved in the local economy and business.[25] Campbell's name occurs quite frequently as a guest in Mr Sanderson's game book.

24. NLS, Acc. 10225, Reclamations, 41, monthly reports on 'Reclamation and Improvement of land at West Shinness in the parish of Lairg.'
25. For instance, in 1889, when J.R. Campbell first took the tenancy of Shinness, he did so jointly with Mr Sanderson, presumably for financial reasons: Acc. 10225, Farms, 41, 'Memorandum of conditions of let of Shinness farm to M.E. Sanderson and J.R. Campbell', 5 Oct. 1889.

Like most of the lodges built on the Sutherland Estate in the later nineteenth century, the estate's official architect at this time, William Fowler, designed and oversaw the construction of Shinness Lodge. Fowler was based in Golspie and handled all of the estate's architectural design and build requirements, from improvements and repairs to new building projects and Dunrobin Castle itself: the rash of lodges built by the estate at this time certainly kept Fowler very busy, as his correspondence books testify.[26] As well as the architectural design of the lodge, Fowler oversaw the practicalities of their build and completion, effectively acting as a modern-day project manager.[27]

The eventful history of Shinness Lodge and farm continued into the twentieth century: the land was sold by the 5th Duke of Sutherland in 1919. In 1922, a 'land settlement scheme' initiated by Lloyd George was carried out on the tenanted farms by the Board of Agriculture for Scotland, although the lodge and sportings were left alone.[28] Under this scheme twenty-nine new tenanted crofts were created on four of the farms, for servicemen returning from the First World War, and these farms and the entire hill land at Shinness Estate and West Shinness Estate were put under 'crofting tenure' for sheep and cattle grazing. Crofting tenure is a specially protected form of permanent agricultural tenancy, leaving the landlord in effect with an interest in

26. NLS, Acc. 10225, Architect's correspondence, 256, William Fowler to John Blake, 30 Jun. 1881; 4 Jul. 1881; 23 Aug. 1881.

27. For example see NLS, Acc. 10225, Architect's correspondence, 258, William Fowler to Edwin Sanderson, 27 Apr. 1883; 21 Aug. 1883; 29 Sept. 1883; 26 Jan. 1884.

28. For a more detailed treatment of the Shinness case, see L. Leneman, *Fit for Heroes? Land Settlement in Scotland after World War One* (Aberdeen, 1989).

the sportings alone. In 1924, the estate was divided into three parts, West Shinness, Shinness and Fiag estates, and each was bought by a different proprietor, Shinness being purchased by George Beldam and West Shinness by Reginald Maudsley.

The biggest change to the appearance of the land, though, came much later in 1954 when, under the 'Power from the Glens' initiative of the post-war Secretary of State, Tom Johnston, a hydro-electric scheme on Loch Shin (one of eleven built at the time) was established, to become fully operational in 1960. It dramatically and permanently changed the landscape, raising the loch by 39 feet and forming a vast reservoir cutting off normal river flow to the sea except for the regular weekly release of 'compensation water'. A small fish pass in each dam was meant to enable fish to get back up the system to the rivers above the Lairg dams. The enlarged loch submerged some of the land laboriously reclaimed by the 3rd Duke's land schemes and flooded large parts of the lower-lying West Shinness Estate.

Shinness has witnessed a varied and eventful modern history. Iby Fraser has ably chronicled her early years as the daughter of one of the first keepers at Shinness, while Ann Gray's survey of the first 100 years of Colaboll gives her perspective as a farmer's daughter. Both Iby and Ann were educated at Edinburgh University and returned to teach at Lairg school for many years. Their memories paint a colourful picture of their lives and the people they knew while growing up in the early twentieth century.

Dr Anne-Marie Tindley
Glasgow Caledonian University
November 2011

Iby Fraser and Her Family, Shinness and Lairg

———— ◆ ————

Isobel Jessie Fraser lived in Main Street, Lairg and was known to everyone throughout her long life as Iby.

Iby was one of a family of four, with an elder sister Anne (known as Daisy), a younger sister Normanna and a brother Simon. All of the children were born at Shinness Lodge in the county of Sutherland between 1898 and 1911 and all attended school in Shinness and then in the nearby village of Lairg.

Their father John Fraser was gamekeeper on Shinness Estate. He was a local man, born on his father's croft at Milnclarin in Lairg in 1863, and his wife Margaret Mac-Donald came from the croft of Knockarthur in Rogart. Sadly, John passed away in 1922 from peritonitis, a condition which could have been addressed by antibiotics had any been available at that time. He left a wife and young family.

Upon leaving school, Daisy attended the Edinburgh College of Domestic Science in Atholl Crescent before undertaking teacher training and qualifying as a Home Economics teacher. She taught initially in Fife, but later moved back to Lairg, teaching in various Sutherland schools.

Daisy married Robert Donald MacDonald from the croft

17

of Knockdhu in Lairg, being affectionately known as 'Mrs RD' locally. Together RD and Daisy managed the Lairg telephone exchange, and were both very involved with local community organisations and initiatives.

Normanna settled in Lairg, marrying John Robb, who worked for the North of Scotland Hydro-Electric Board at the Loch Shin Dam.

Simon followed in his father's footsteps and trained as a gamekeeper, working with Lairg Estate, and served with the RAF during the Second World War. Later he worked for Colonel Whitbread on Letterewe Estate in Ross-shire, and he and his wife Beatrice (Nan) both remained in the Whitbreads' employment until retirement.

Iby completed her schooling in Lairg and went on to take an MA (Hons) degree in English at Edinburgh University in 1924, followed by a teaching diploma. This was quite an achievement for a young girl in those days and her family were rightly proud of her. For a year after graduating, Iby was a relief teacher in Lochinver and at Sutherland Technical College, after which she obtained a permanent position in Lairg, where she remained for her entire teaching career, much of this as Infant Mistress. Generations of children attending Lairg school benefited from her good humour and her infectious love of learning.

Iby's commitment to the Lairg community had a broad base. She was in the Church of Scotland choir for over 50 years and was a member of the Presbyterial Council and Women's Guild. As a long-term and latterly honorary member of the Lairg SWRI, Iby gave occasional talks to the group about her life and experiences. This led her to transcribe her 'Memories of a Highland Girlhood in 1900' in the 1970s for Margaret Fletcher, who herself lived at Shinness Lodge for nearly 50 years.

Iby Fraser's manuscript, 'A Wisp of History', explaining the derivation of 'Lairg' as a place-name. 'Shinness', which predates Lairg as a settlement, may have Norse roots rather than Gaelic ones.

Reclamation works at Colaboll in the 1870s.

Reclamation works etching from Dunrobin Castle with the 'Duke's Toothpick' in the foreground. The kilted figure may be the Duke of Sutherland.

Monument to Kenneth Murray of Geanies as it is today.

The Duke's luncheon house on Loch Shin as it is today.

Daisy and Iby Fraser and Feannach the dog.

Above. John and Margaret Fraser with Daisy and Iby at the Keeper's House, Shinness Lodge, *c.* 1908.

Right. John Fraser, Iby's father.

Margaret Fraser, Iby's mother.

Iby Fraser at the gate of her house, Lovatlea, Main Street, Lairg in 1980.

Uncle Donald, Normanna, Daisy, Iby and Bob Munro.

The coming of the car – at the Sutherland Arms Hotel Lairg, around 1911.

J. R. Campbell's car, with number plate still in use by the Campbell family.

Taking home the peats, with Ben More Assynt in the background.

Tinkers' encampment near Loch Shin.

Tinkers on the road in the 1930s.

Shooting party at Shinness on the Aird in the 1920s.

Looking west towards Shinness Farm (now West Shinness Lodge) from the Aird in the 1920s, on ground now flooded.

E.	DISTRICT.	No. of Guns.	Grouse (Brace).	Black Game.	Wild Duck.	Snipe.	Hares.	Sundries.
1906.								
1.	Above & below Loch Vacavie	2.				7.	6	
7	do.	2.				3	5	
9	Shot for. the House		4 4		by Fraser	1 Wigeon		
13.	By Tury Side & End of Aird		14½	5				2.
14	opposite to Green. Hill & Tury Side	Kn C	13				1	1
15	At Sion R from Hill & Blar Beni	2	21.			1	1	
16	By. side of Loch Shin	3	18	2.				
17	By Loch Shin se & Midperny	4	20½	7				
18	Loch Shin Side & by Vacavie	4	25½	13			3	
20	Above & below Loch Vacavie			3		5	1	
21	Tallich. & Aird by Woods.	4	23 22	1		1	1	
22.	Left Sior "Alt na Suarach		25				1	
23	By. Alt na Guarach.		12½	5				
.	opposite by Loch Shin		20½				1	
25	m Road leading to Aird		1 Roebuck					
.	by Burn do		1 do					
	m & about Blas Buie		10½	1 OB. Jame			3.	
	TOTAL		212	46	11	18	14	2

A page from M.E. Sanderson's game book, noting MES and Fraser as guns.

this year the first

Partridges.	Pheasants.	Rabbits.	Total.	REMARKS.
			13.	Guns M⟨ES⟩ & Fraser.
				Do Do
			1.	Guns Copeland, Kenyon & M E S
				Do Do Do.
				Do Do Do & Guy Leatham
				Guy Leatham
				Col. C. & M⟨rs⟩.
				Guy L. & Mr Kenyon
				Guy Leatham
				Kenyon.
1				
1		1		2 Roebuck

Shooting party on Cnoc an Ulbhaidh, Shinness with Ben Klibreck in the background.

House party at Shinness Lodge in 1920s, guests seated with keepers at the back and house staff on the right, with chauffeur in peaked cap at front.

Colaboll Farm before the First World War, with Alec Gray as a boy, on the left.

Some members of the Gray family with guests at Colaboll on a special occasion, probably 'The Sacraments' in Lairg Free Church, around the mid 1930s. Ann Gray is standing behind the seated baby, with her mother Mary standing to her left behind the minister. Malcolm is mid-way between them standing at the back, and Alec is standing at the right of the window.

Graduation portrait of
Ann Gray.

Ann Gray.

Having been brought up on a sporting estate, Iby's love for the wildlife and landscape of Scotland, and for family and friends, remained with her. This can be seen clearly in her writing within this book, where she records through a child's eyes and with great affection the day-to-day duties and activities of her family and acquaintances 100 years ago.

Iby passed away on 30 December 1994 shortly after her 90th birthday. She left behind a lifetime of paperwork, family photographs and correspondence which mirror her long and happy life, some of which are reproduced here.

Recollections of Highland Childhood

by Iby Fraser

———— ✦ ————

Keeper's House Shinness Lodge
Lairg
Sutherland
Sunday

Dear Mrs Fletcher

Last year I promised I'd write out for you the little bits and pieces I'd put together for the SWRI evening Ann [Gray], Mrs Ross [Tirryside] and I 'had' for recollections.

Here they are then – and I hope you will not be bored reading them. My writing too is decidedly not of the best and for that I apologise. Just burn the 'epistle' when finished – I've a copy worse than this, be it said, for myself.

I could have added more – but enough is enough and I had to be in the mood, because otherwise it was an effort and I wanted to enjoy the doing of it – so it was an occasional pastime.

I wonder how Homer felt when he finished *The Iliad*? No – really the 'Village Blacksmith' – 'something attempted, something done has earned a night's repose' – so I learned in school. It is now midnight, so I hope repose follows my lying down to rest!

Love from Iby

p.s. The names of friends are all fictional because some – or their offspring – are alive today and I wouldn't want you to know them or you might smile when next you saw them. I changed our own family's names too – to conform![29]

p.p.s Please excuse mistakes!

Aye dear to me . . .

Summer afternoon sunshine streaming through a sky-light window onto an upstairs landing found me, Iby Fraser, nearly three years old, attempting to cling – in vain – to a newel post, as my fat little fingers could not possibly stretch far enough to encompass its girth. The consequence? A few faltering steps on the varnished stair edges, not on the hair carpet, as I was too frightened to leave what I thought was the safety of the wall – and then, blessed oblivion! I had gone headlong round the curve of the stairway across the passage below, my forehead hitting the bolt that secured the foot of the 'middle' door – and that was that.

Consternation ensued. My father, mother and elder sister Daisy were having afternoon tea downstairs by the fire while the baby, Normanna, sat up in her cradle, but my scream put an end to their happy conversation.

Of course, I was only momentarily stunned, but everyone was shocked and my father, who had intended going to the church service held monthly in the nearby little school, stayed anxiously at home.

The cause of my downfall was a pair of beautiful, new

---

29. Given that some 40 years have passed since Iby set down her recollections, names have been changed back to real ones.

buttoned brown boots. They came from Bayne & Duckett Glasgow (still in business), and their soles were highly polished. I was too young to think of the danger awaiting my unwary feet when I started off downstairs on my own.

I remember the brown stockings I wore too – fine cotton they were, ribbed, with lacy 'clocks' at the ankles, and they had elastic hoops at the top attached to suspenders fixed to my liberty bodice. Our underwear came from Price Jones, Newtown, North Wales, though some things, for example our petticoats, were handmade and embroidered by my mother. My dress was of fine blue cashmere, fashioned by her clever hands too, and over it I wore a white, starched pinafore with frills at the yoke and hem. My hair hung free, except for the front, which was scooped up, plaited and tied with a blue silk ribbon.

After this episode, my father fixed gates at the top and bottom of the stairs to prevent further accidents – and that is as far back in my life as I can remember today.

I was always the child who was afraid – and I don't know how or why. Where my sisters, specially Normanna, were never scared of tackling anything, I used to lag behind – to see what happened.

Our home was in Shinness, where my father John Fraser was head keeper. Trees – birch, sycamore, firs and different species, beech, the occasional lime, laburnum and rowan (or mountain ash) surrounded it. I loved to hear the wind howling through the bare branches in winter, and soughing softly when the leaves were green in summer.

A burn ran from the rear of the shooting lodge – about a quarter of a mile that building was from our home – past the back of our larder, and what fun we had playing there! We leapt across it when it was trickling, we plopped stones into it when the water ran level – bank to bank – and we stared at it, fascinated, when it was a miniature torrent, foam-flecked and angry.

The foam, as the current subsided, drifted slowly to the sides of the burn and that, when we played 'houses', was our whipped cream. It stayed stiff for ages and had a lovely texture.

My father built us a wooden summer house at the foot of our garden, made a nice wide seat all round inside its three walls, and a cupboard for our dishes. Hops at the back made a fine green covering, falling partly over the roof. We had a swing between a sycamore and a lime tree where the bees hummed – drowsily to us – above our heads and it had a wooden seat where two of us could sit side by side and while away the hours with deep enjoyment. I can still see, in my mind's eye, the hollow bare of grass made by our feet as we levered ourselves off the ground. I never of course liked to swing too high. Going up was a delight but coming down was dreadful so I just drifted slowly up and down again – dreading a push from behind!

The same feeling overwhelmed me when, as an adult, I was descending Glamaig[30] on Skye after an arduous climb and a magnificent view over the Cuillin to the mainland and the Outer Hebrides. At one stage, like the Grand Old Duke of York, stuck neither up nor down – unwilling to move – I was literally petrified, but with a good arm to grip mine, I came back eventually to the lower slopes. Funnily enough, though often sailing over rough seas I was never seasick.

My sister Normanna and I were like twins because only two years separated our birthdays. We slept together when we were old enough to do so. Before that, Normanna

30. At 775m, the highest point of Skye's Red Hills.

occupied the family cradle, a beautiful basketwork one with thick rockers, the hood padded by my skilful mother with cotton wool, then covered with rosebud-scattered and be-ribboned patterned cretonne.

All that time, I slept in a camp bed against the bedroom wall and, so that I didn't hurt my head, my mother padded and covered a part of the wall just as she had the cradle. When I stretched up my arms I loved to touch it!

Our perambulator was blue too – soft leather, covered in basketry, with shafts, and had two big and two small wheels. When I could be trusted to do so, I used to wheel my little brother Simon around the premises – he was much younger than we were – and very important I felt too.

His christening robe was of fine lawn with dozens of tucks down the wide tapering front, feather stitched and with a deep embroidered hem. A long blue cloak, with silk lining, was worn with it.

Our windows slid open to the side and we had a delightful view of the loch a short distance away. We often saw anglers there, flicking their rods over the rippling and maybe calm waters, though that was a sport I never all my long life fancied.

When I grew strong enough, I learned how to row a boat and never really tired of *that*, but was hard put to it to keep quiet when my father was fishing. He himself was not over-fond of the pastime either, to tell the truth, much preferring to go shooting. Nevertheless, the sound of water lapping against the boat or the plopping of the trout did make me happy.

Smells have played a great part in my memories and I can conjure up at will the fresh scent – for that's what it was – of the loch, the pungent odour of the hot tar and paint of the boat on a sunny day, while from the shore came the perfume of bog myrtle or clover, as the case may be. The rattle of the anchor chain seemed to sound different too when one was actually *on* the water. It had a softer sound than when the boat was being hauled ashore.

Sporting Life

Our home was a very happy one and our whole lives centred round our beloved parents. My father was slightly built, very active, always whistling from morning until night unless he was out on the hills – and rarely, if ever, was he angry. I never met anyone so full of goodwill and the joy of life as he was, even when he must have been dog-tired – for there were no 'days off' in my childhood.

During the shooting season, when the tenants occupied the lodge, the working week was a seven day one, but I never heard him or the under keeper or any of the ghillies grumble. The weather was the only thing that troubled them – apart from the midges. Clegs were a nuisance too, but then these pests are universal in the Highlands. We did not like the bats that fluttered round the house in the gloaming either.

The shooting tenants took over the lodge at the beginning of August but, before their arrival, the private road was hoed, gravelled and raked to perfection. The garage (at one time coach house) was cleared thoroughly and the young fry supplied with old knives to clean between the cobblestones which lay before the building. Every corner was spick and span and the housekeeper at the lodge – she lived there permanently – had someone to help her spring clean. The whole place became a hive of industry, with a cook, kitchen maid, scullery maid, butler, table maid, housemaids, valets, ladies' maids, coachmen (latterly chauffeurs), ghillies, gun-dogs and horses.

All seemed happy. That was the way of life and there did not seem to be any hurry. Time, except for trains, meals and meetings, was of no importance.

The twelfth of August was a great day. Stout garrons[31] had panniers strapped to their saddles and with double-barrelled guns, spying glasses (telescopes) and coupled pointers and setters at heel, the shooting party set off to the hills accompanied by keepers and ghillies, and with packed lunches and leather-covered glass and silver flasks of whisky, the atmosphere was one of enthusiastic anticipation. As the afternoon wore on, the cavalcade returned in time to dress for dinner – panniers laden with grouse, black game, partridges, woodcock, hares, etc. which were hung up in the big larder at the lodge. The guns were meticulously cleaned with ramrods or pull-throughs and wrapped in oily tow, ready for the following day.

Later in the season came the deer stalking – with horses specially trained to carry the stags on deer saddles. This was a lengthier day, but usually just as rewarding.

No one minded being soaked to the skin, or plastered in wet peaty mire, if the 'stalk' was on such ground.

The stags, or hinds latterly, were hung up in the larder, weighed and skinned, and everything tidied up in readiness for the next day's sport before the keepers retired to their homes and the ghillies to their 'ghillie-room' – really a little house with a kitchen and open fireplace at one end, and a bedroom at the other – snug and wood-lined. (The ghillies cooked their own meals and washed their clothes if they were unable to go home for weekends; over the years, many a name was carved on the kitchen wall!)

---

31. A small sturdy type of horse, used especially for rough hill work.

The arrival of motors

Mail for the lodge was collected in a private bag from the seven-mile-distant Lairg Post Office on every day of the week, Sunday included. For the rest of the year, until the First World War ended, we ourselves met the mail-car at the foot of our road, in the forenoon, as it made its way to the villages on the west coast. If letters had to be posted, we returned in the afternoon and met another mail-car making for Lairg.

Mostly the vehicles were Albions – open-fronted, no cab for shelter – with sides like present day stock lorries, though not so closely shuttered. There was no roof to such a contraption, and if there were more passengers than two who could squeeze in beside the driver, they had to clamber up over the wooden frame at the rear. If children were travelling they were literally hauled up aloft by their arms.

In winter the driver wore two coats, at least – like an onion, he was! – and a balaclava helmet, with usually a drip to his nose.

As time passed the mail contractors purchased small buses with proper seats for passengers – something like a glorified shooting-brake – and with a covered cab for the driver. A canvas hood stretched over the passengers and the occasional 'bagged'[32] calf, as well as the mail bags.

When we were small there were various conveyances on the estate, for example buggies, as light as a feather, that could easily be pulled by a strong man. They had four high wheels and seats for two over each pair of wheels, facing forwards. Many a ride Normanna and I had behind a stout chauffeur's back in wartime! There was a wagonette, with brakes and socket for whip, whose seats could be lowered to

32. Animals were constrained in this way when carried with passengers.

take luggage instead of passengers, or dogs to the hill if the shoot was on a far beat.

A favourite 'horse' of ours was an Austrian chauffeur who willingly pulled the buggy. His dressing-set – in his bedroom behind the gun-room – was gold-mounted, better than that of his master, who was a captain in the Black Watch and billeted at a nearby camp. He only came home at the weekends, so didn't have much time for sport.

The chauffeur was later interned as a spy, much to our chagrin, but I think to my mother's relief, as he was a giant of a man and she feared for our safety because the Lairg policeman cycled to Shinness each week to interview him – making the poor chap quite angry!

The coming of the motorcar to the lodge was a red-letter day in our lives. I can still remember the smell of the sun-warmed leather upholstery and the petrol fumes on a summer morning when the kindly chauffeur bundled Normanna and me – coats over our night dresses – in beside him as he drove away to one of the crofts for the household's milk. Before his advent, an odd-boy used to whizz away on his bicycle, with pails clanking, on the same errand. Many a spill he had – not necessarily of milk – and how we laughed! But he took us in turn, on the crossbar, for a little way when fetching the afternoon supply, and how thrilled we were!

John Fraser

When out with a shooting party, my father always kept the cakes from his packed lunch for us supplied by the kitchen staff. He just ate the sandwiches. That was typical of him. Everything he could do for the happiness and welfare of his children was a joy to him. He whistled in the mornings when he set off to the kennels or the lodge, and at nights, tired though he undoubtedly was, he still whistled a merry tune.

He was a member of the Lairg Black and White Minstrels show and of the County Volunteers Pipe Band, being often called to play at events in the village. In fact, just before he died, he, with a fellow piper, played the lament – the Flowers of the Forest – when the parish war memorial was unveiled. It could well have been his own death dirge, my well-beloved.

Nursery rhymes

Gamekeepers' wives in those days always had a girl to help in the house, and we were blessed with two or three at different times who sang like linties.[33] Often we learned songs which we couldn't understand, and which were perhaps not in the best of taste, but my mother, being a wise woman, knew that we would forget them in the passage of time, remembering only melodies, so she never interfered. '*Green grow the laurels, soft falls the dew . . .*' and '*I wish, I wish, but I wish in vain, I wish I were a maid again . . .*' were two of them which folksingers have brought back to popularity today after all those years.

That was the way with swear words too. Occasionally, one of the ghillies, exasperated, would vent his feelings about a bothersome horse or dog in an expression unfit for children's ears, but that was seldom, for they were circumspect when we were around; but if the off word did slip out, we ran home directly calling, 'Mammie, we learned a new word today.' She would say, 'Oh did you?' We burst forth with the – to us – wonderful acquisition and all she'd say was, 'Well, well.' And that was that. No excitement and we were deflated, and the word died a natural death.

---

33. Linnets.

Mother taught us rhymes and sang jingles – and how we loved them: for example

Clap handies, clap handies till daddy comes home.
Daddy has money but Mammie has more.

Knock at the door [tap forehead]
peep in [lift eyelid gently]
lift the latch [tip up the nose]
and walk in [pretend to put finger in child's mouth].

This little piggy went to market;
this little piggy stayed at home;
this little piggy had roast beef;
this little piggy had none;
and this little piggy said 'wee wee wee' [high pitched voice]
  all the way home.

This she played with our tiny toes.

Crippled Dick upon a stick, Sandy on one too.
Rode away to Galloway, for a pound of glue.

Here we go round the Juga-rig, Juga-rig, Juga-rig
  [one of us in the middle of the ring]
Here we go round the Juga-rig, around the merry-ma-tanzie.

London Bridge is falling down . . .

By putting her hands together, and letting them fall to her knees one by one, she made the sound of a horse walking or galloping, according to the speed she used, saying – *'Peter Dick, Peter Dick'*. By interlacing our fingers and turning them palms upwards, we said – '*Here's the lady's knives and forks*'. Then keeping the same position but turning our backs of the hands upwards, '*Here's the lady's table.*' With two little fingers erect – '*Here's the lady's looking glass*', and now holding thumbs upright as well as little fingers – '*Here's the baby's cradle; rick rock rick rock*'. And we rocked our hands to and fro. We rode '*a cock horse to Banbury Cross*' on her leg or my father's, while he often carried us pick-a-back as he went from building to building.

School

Before being enrolled at school at seven years of age – I refused point-blank to go until Normanna could come too – I knew my alphabet and was able to read reasonably well for my age, having been taught by my father and mother. We had both played with lettered blocks at home and had linen books with pictures of birds and animals whose names began with the different letters of the alphabet, so she as well as I were not unprepared for what lay before us. My tears and supplication had benefited me, but it was a long, long walk for my little sister, the pretty wee mite, as we set out for school with my father taking us either side by the hand. It was just after Normanna's fifth birthday and the walk continued for over two and a half miles. A car would have been provided by the Education Committee today!

We soon settled down in this new world, but the long walk proved too far for Normanna – although the shepherd's sons carried her part of the way home – and she became ill.

We had endless poems to learn – by Shelley, Keats, Wordsworth, Browning, Tennyson, etc., together with chosen passages from the Old and New Testaments and many psalms. These I recall, in part, to this day and with multiplication tables, weights and measures, length etc., our memories were well taxed and gave us a good start for our entry into any walk of life.

I well remember the cruelty of our first teacher on occasion. We had copy books to improve our writing skill and before Normanna had advanced to this stage, she was given single letters and words to write in a jotter. On one particular day the word was 'dog' and she wrote on the last part of the page the word 'god'. For that she was punished – two strokes of the strap or belt across the hot stove, teacher on one side, child on the other. Unintentional though it was, the blows on the little palms forced Normanna's hand onto the stove lid and a blister appeared, red and angry. Naturally, she began to cry and so did I, so we were both banished to the porch, to cling together, sobbing among the rows of wet coats. The school house was attached to the school and the teacher's mother, who stayed with her, heard our crying. She came to comfort us, taking us into her warm kitchen and saying, 'Wait till your teacher comes in.' We knew she got a real scolding – we'd each got a sweetie! – because she took a pill of some kind back to school with her and a glass of water. Quite obviously she hadn't had her elevenses *that* day.

One good thing about her apart from her beauty was that she played the harmonium (her own property) as she accompanied our singing.

When this teacher resigned, her successor was quite a different personality. She was full of kindness and was very vivacious. She made the more difficult lessons seem pleasant. We hurried to school in the mornings so that we could run to meet her as she cycled during the summer from Lairg. She taught us how to paint. Our paint boxes had little cubes of different colours and had hollows in the lids where we mixed the paints with water. We modelled with clay – I can smell it still! – and she taught us to sing rounds and duets. We pressed leaves, glued them into a plain-leaved writing jotter, then varnished them, adding the name of each species. Sometimes we were lucky enough to find skeleton leaves in the wood. These were absolutely wonderful in their fragile intricacy.

One snag – there is always a thorn among the roses – was the teacher's cairn terrier. It used to sneak through the open door on sunny days while we were out of doors at play and steal the 'piece' from someone's bag. Then of course we shared what we had to eat with the unfortunate victim.

We sat at long desks on seats which accommodated four children and those desks were well carved with the names of pupils who had sat behind them for many, many years before. We used slates and squeaking slate pencils with little pieces of sponge attached by string to a hole at the top of the frame. Sometimes we used water, sometimes we spat on them – hygiene? The boys in a hurry used their sleeves many a time to dry their slates and were smacked for messing up their jackets.

At break time we skipped, played 'housie meetie', an intricate form of rounders, and we drilled like soldiers on the grassy playground. That is why I still squirm when I see Cubs, Brownies or Guides marching out of step today. Even as adults, we automatically matched our steps to our companions', as that was instilled into us from early childhood.

At lunch time, the teacher made cocoa in a big enamelled jug and poured it into small mugs for each child. We drank it with sandwiches and cakes and biscuits which we had carried from home. Later on, when Thermos flasks came onto the market, we brought tea in our school bags.

In the primary school a half-day's holiday was only given

when the Inspector came for our annual examination. If questions were answered intelligently, and copy books neat, we were told to go home and enjoy ourselves for the rest of the day. What relief, and delight!

At the Higher Grade School, pupils who could not go home for a meal at midday got soup in the winter from the school soup kitchen to which the farmers and crofters sent gifts of potatoes, carrots and turnips. Estate proprietors gifted hinds which the local butcher cut up, salted and delivered to the cook as required. Rabbits were often sent too, so that all that had to be bought were cereals, onions and leeks. Any leftovers were sent in a bucket daily across the field to my granny's pig – a welcome gift indeed.

School concerts were held to pay for the upkeep of the soup kitchen – wages, etc. – and these were the highlight of the year. What a lot of work went into the effort from infants upwards. The infant teacher taught singing and sewing as well to all the school. How she did it I know not, but the strap and pointer were part and parcel of her methods.

Some of the fair-haired or red-haired children at the school had lovely skin sprinkled with freckles – 'fairy kisses' – and the boys called these little spots 'ferntickles',[34] as they called earwigs 'forky tails'. One boy used to say 'I'll go my lone' instead of 'alone' and that had a much more expressive sense of isolation – a sadness about it.

Winter

When snowflakes fell softly from the sky, my mother used to say, 'They're plucking the geese in Caithness' – a lovely thought. Once when our daddy came home on such a day

---

34. Or fairnytickles.

after taking the kennel dogs for a walk – the under keeper being in the trenches in France at the time, from which he never returned, dear lad that he was – he said, 'I've seen an unforgettable sight this day!' A long snowstorm had just come to an end and 'spirits' had run out at one inn some distance away. So a shepherd who was a regular – and now disappointed – customer felt so desperate in so far as his thirst was concerned that he removed the bottom parts with the castors off his rocking chair and harnessed his horse to this makeshift sleigh. My father couldn't make out what was approaching him and nearly fell over with laughter when the contraption came up to him. The old man had his legs swathed in straw and his body well wrapped up in a cloak, while a cap with 'ears' completed his outfit.

We had a sleigh ourselves and sometimes drove to Lairg in it, imagining being Santa Clauses as the snow sprayed up from the runners. When the sun was shining, as it usually was when we set out, the scenery was really glorious. The snow-capped hills and hillocks seemed rainbow-hued, the trees like those on Christmas cards and the air intoxicating. We were well clad to keep out the cold with hoods and scarves and coats made by the Lairg tailor.

Once, this man arrived at our house for a coat fitting. He came on his bicycle, on Christmas Eve, after a day's work, only to find us a-bed. While we were called downstairs we could hardly wait to have pins stuck here and there in the cut-out tweed, lest Santa visit our bedroom and find us gone.

Before motor cars took over, we had the roads to ourselves, more or less. The horse's breath rose in little warm puffs and its ears were cocked as it looked from side to side enjoying itself mightily – especially on its way home. The only trouble we encountered was on passing a farm where often pigs strayed into the ditches and then the horse had to be coaxed and led past the offending animals. That was quite a difficult task, as horses do not like pigs, smelling them some distance away and stopping dead in their tracks.

Our parents wore coats with capes for travelling and we had rugs of a strong, soft, waterproof material lined with checked flannel or the like. The rugs had a ring inserted in a heart-shaped plaque near the top so that one could hold them up after tucking them snugly round one's body. Normanna and I sometimes wore fur necklets and muffs – always to church in winter – the muffs hanging round our necks on twisted silken cords. Normanna had a beautiful little white fur cap with a fox's head – bright yellow-eyed on the side – with necklet and muff to match.

Family and food

We always visited my granny's house when in Lairg. That was my father's home, my maternal granny having died when we were very young. There the horse was stabled, fed and watered while our parents went about their business. Granny spoiled us and never let us leave, after a good meal of course, without some little gift, perhaps an egg spoon or the like for each of us. She was a bonnie little woman who wore a white goffered[35] mutch,[36] blue-tinted glasses and a blue and white print apron. She had a comfy lap to sit on too. Her fireplace was low and had white pipe-clayed sides where her cats sat and purred. A crook or swey[37] that had a chain with hooks attached swung out well over the fire, carrying black iron kettles or three-legged pots. She, like us,

---

35. Crimped or fluted.
36. Linen cap.
37. A movable iron bar.

burned peats. The fireplace had a flap below the cross-bars which she lifted at night and, after having placed peats standing up across the flat bars, she took a shovel of ashes from below and after placing a big, wettish peat across the construction, she 'smoored' or smothered the fire. In the morning, she just lifted off the top peat, which had lain horizontally all night, and up came the flames. The fire never went out except when the chimney had to be cleaned. That was done from the top with a heather brush, weighted with lead, dropped down and pulled up again and again. Granny had a pot oven, too, in which she baked delicious cakes. It had a flat iron lid and, after putting the cake in the tin inside the big pot, she put red-hot embers on the lid so that the baking was done from above as well as from beneath.

I never tasted shop cakes, except my brother's christening cake, in my own home as everything was home-baked. Strangely enough, most of us really appreciated this until we grew up and had the baker's variety. Lairg, incidentally, had a very good baker, Mr Watt. His wife was equally good, but she had a fiery temper and we were afraid of her when we were old enough to do the shopping ourselves.

When making scones, Granny always went to the open outer door with the bowl of flour and, lifting the meal high in her hand, let it trickle through her fingers so that it was thoroughly aerated, giving a delightfully light scone which kept fresh for days. Her oatcakes were lovely too, but I preferred my mother's, which were thinner than hers and 'curled'. Both women toasted their oatcakes in front of the fire after having baked them on the girdle. Mother's toaster hung on the bars of the range and had holes so that the upright support could be moved backwards and forwards depending on the intensity of the heat of the fire. Granny's stood in front of the fireplace with a brick supporting it.

She and later my auntie made 'Crappit Heids' – fish heads stuffed with a mixture of oatmeal, suet, chopped fish livers, onion and seasonings. Greaseproof paper was tied securely round the heads and they were simmered gently. A more tasty dish one cannot imagine. In after years, I asked my auntie why she had stopped making this for dinner and her reply was, 'You don't see haddies with big enough heads nowadays!' We used to get herring too, and scaled, gutted and split them, frying them fresh in oatmeal, potting them in vinegar, seasoning and a little water, and steaming them. On occasion we salted them, laying them side by side and head to tail in a pudding dish and leaving them for perhaps a week. Boiled gently and eaten with plain boiled potatoes, they were a treat. I much preferred them done so to the salt herring sold from barrels, which always were dry and hard, as well as being too salty. We used to develop a real thirst after a midday meal of the latter type, but my uncle vowed that if we took a milk pudding thereafter our thirst would be speedily and effectively quenched. How right he was.

I remember some years ago visiting Mallaig when the drifters were in port unloading herring and my friend said to one old man hauling up the baskets, 'That's what makes brains!'

'Not at all,' he replied, 'It's the water you drink after eating them!'

Speldings, that is haddock that has been split and smoked, would often be made by fishwives. These hardy women came to Lairg by the morning train with heavy creels of fish and sold them throughout the parish. While they waited at the railway station for the evening train home, they gathered cones from the fir wood nearby and filled up their creels. That was the material they used for smoking their haddock and cod in the sheds behind their houses. They smoked herring into kippers, too.

Milk puddings were usually made from rice, sago or barley (called 'stoved' barley), or junket made from fresh milk, rennet, sugar and vanilla essence, served with cream when available. Granny just made curds and whey – no sugar or essence – and that we did not like. She made a very nice pudding with rhubarb, stewed with sugar and poured hot into a bowl lined with slices of bread. The bowl was lightly greased, and she put slices of bread (crusts removed, of course) across the top, then placed a weighted plate over all. Next day she turned it out – a jellied pudding. Delicious! The rhubarb was flavoured with cloves.

Mother made steamed puddings, too, and roly-polies with jam, and we often had jelly and custard. Our schoolboy friends once told us that sago was dried frogspawn and that put us off sago pudding for long enough. After the first milking, when a cow calved, my auntie made 'beestings' from the next milking. She put the milk in a cinnamon-bottomed tin like a loaf tin, added sugar, steamed it and then turned it out on an ashette – a creamy brown-topped mound. If I didn't know what it was, I'd have enjoyed it more – but I ate the cinnamon top with no bother at all. Babies were given saps made of bread and milk, rusks soaked in warm milk, or baby porridge – oatmeal mixed with milk to a paste, hot water added, the mixture strained and the thin liquid sweetened and boiled up. Rich Tea biscuits were sometimes crushed and had hot milk added as a change from ordinary saps. My mother always added a little salt to her milk puddings, as this greatly improved the flavour of an otherwise pallid dish.

Hens and eggs

We had quite a number of hens – Rhode Island Reds, Minorcans and Barred Rocks – and one of our duties was to clear the hen house. A china, really clay, egg was put in each nest to induce the hens to lay. A little ladder, a solid affair – led up to the spars, or perches, where the hens roosted, and the wooden floor beneath was covered liberally with hay and bracken.

Whenever we heard a hen cackle, we rushed to collect the egg, though sometimes we waited until late afternoon when we might get a basketful.

Often, the hens laid away in summer – among the trees or bracken – and if we found a nest with a goodly number of eggs, we filled a basin with water and popped the eggs in. If they floated, they were addled, and *our* property! Those that sank were reserved and delivered to the house, but the 'floaters' we took behind the kennels, where there was a spring clay-pigeon 'trap'. We carefully put our eggs into the cup, pulled back the spring, and off the egg shot, spraying its odorous contents into the air. The pleasure that gave us really surmounted the terrific aroma that surrounded us!

When hens became broody, we called them 'clockers' – probably that should have been 'cluckers', because they clucked all the time and refused to move from their nests.

Some we set on thirteen eggs (always that number, for some unknown reason) and we often wrote our names on them, waiting patiently for three weeks to see whose were the first to hatch – if hatch they did – in a snug, hay-lined wooden box with slatted front. One slat was wider than the others, so that the hen could emerge to feed, drink and have an earth bath – this last she thoroughly enjoyed, fluffing out her feathers and stretching her wings and legs. When the chickens appeared, they were able to come out from the box through the smaller apertures, while Mamma had perforce to stay imprisoned – until they were strong enough to roam around a little, when the hen was permitted to take her

41

brood – so proudly – to the nearest dust bath and scratch to her heart's content – scattering the little creatures with a swipe from her foot – unintentionally, of course.

If we had too many 'clockers', the surplus was confined in upturned wooden boxes – wooden boxes being plentiful then – until they 'cooled'. (Not really upturned, I should say, but placed upside down, with a brick or stone on top.) It was really a drastic punishment, for the poor fowls had no food or drink for a few days. Sometimes, instead, they were 'dooked'[38] in a bucket of cold water – enough to cool animal or human being, I should think, because of the sudden shock! Neighbours of ours put their 'clockers' in hessian bags and let them swing on a clothesline. Mortals can be quite cruel – unwittingly.

During the 1914–18 war, pupils in our little school collected eggs for the war wounded in hospitals and packing them in 30 dozen wooden boxes with padlocks. We wrote our names and addresses on some of the eggs and later received letters of thanks, as we did when we enclosed little 'get-well' messages in our best writing (ah me!!) in the toe of a sock or sewn to a scarf knitted for the troops.

Sphagnum moss[39] we gathered too and many a bag carefully cleaned of twigs, heather or minute pebbles was sent from our school to a central point for distribution to hospitals near the front. How proud we were then, when our teacher read out letters of thanks from those in authority there!

To come back to hens, they were shut in a yard when the garden was flourishing; that is, a yard attached to the hen house. Hens and gardeners don't mix – in the gardeners'

38. Ducked.
39. Used as a dressing for wounds.

42

opinions, at least. However, very often a cabbage at which they could peck was suspended from a rod across the yard. They also got roughage to produce strong-shelled eggs, and this was from broken stone jam-jars, easily come-by in those days, which were finely smashed for the hens.

Keepers pierced eggs and inserted strychnine to kill that menace the hoodie crow and, yes, the black-backed gull. The eggs were placed on an island in the loch, well away from the attention of domestic cats or dogs, and any other animal that might be attracted. The hoodie was mercilessly pursued all the year round and shot on sight. If one was seen, it was a black mark against the keeper on that beat because there were no vacant tenancies in those days, nor were there nature reserves, which can be so good in many ways, but a nursery, I think – however careful the wardens may be – for many predators. Farmers, keepers and shepherds, no doubt, will be of the same mind as I.

When eggs were plentiful, my mother preserved quite a goodly number in water glass for winter use, and when she removed them from the crock, they had little white 'clouds' attached to them, fascinating us, until she washed them ready for use. When the crocks were empty, the remaining liquid was used for washing the kitchen flagstones and those around the porch, as it made them cleaner than anything else. Milk gave the flags a polish.

At Easter, we boiled our eggs with coffee or onion skins, or coloured them with cochineal.

Eggs were bartered for household necessities when the grocer's van paid its weekly visit, so it paid to keep the hens well fed on potatoes mashed with Indian corn for one feed per day, the other consisting of oats. When eggs were plentiful, Mother made lemon curd, of which we were *very* fond.

Produce

Jam was made in a highly polished, slightly greased brass pan. When the season's crop of berries was finally preserved, the pan was polished and greased ready for next year. We had gooseberries, raspberries, rhubarb and blackcurrants in our garden and Granny gave us redcurrants. The gift was made into the most delicious jelly, without cooking. The berries were heated gently in the oven, as was the sugar, and the juice squeezed out into a basin through a jelly bag. The warmed sugar was now added and we took it in turn to stir the lot with a wooden spoon – in *one* direction – until it jelled. It was the actual bright natural colour of the berries and was tart as well as sweet, and very stiff.

Each year my mother made potpourri and I have some still, just as sweetly scented as when she filled the jar. She made all her mincemeat long before Christmas and stored it in a 'two eared' crock, earthenware, cream inside and brown outside. This same type was used for salting down butter for winter use, and when the butter from such a vessel was taken to the table, it lay on a little plate in swirls, having been creamed off with a wooden, serrated curved knife. Butter and cheese were made by every crofter's wife – and farmers' dairy maids – the making of butter being a weekly task. Cream was skimmed off the milk with a perforated metal (tin) skimmer and slid into a big crock, where it waited until it soured. Then into the churn it went – a wooden affair, like the knife machine – and the handle turned rhythmically until the butter 'came'.

Then the buttermilk was drained from the churn and kept for baking, drinking or supping with porridge. Taken this latter way, we dipped our spoonful of porridge into our individual wee bowls of buttermilk and it was a most appetising dish. This was the way Granny had us eat our porridge with fresh milk. She strained the milk into a bowl for each of us after the last milking of the day and covered each bowl with a saucer. They lay in an orderly row on her dresser until the morning – when cream had formed on the top, ready for breakfast. At home we just 'turned up' our porridge, leaving enough space on the plate in which to pour the required amount of milk from a big jug.

In winter time, when the cows were 'dry', we had porter with our porridge. Each autumn, a man arrived with a horse-drawn cart and barrels of porter, selling it from house to house. We put some spoonfuls of sugar on our porridge plates, where we usually poured the milk, melted it with boiling water and added porter. It was very good indeed. Porter with sugar, hot water and a little added oatmeal was a favourite drink, too, among menfolk on a cold day.

Cheese was made from sour milk – a milk soured with rennet. The milk was heated slowly in a pan, away from the fire, at the back of the range, until it thickened into a curd. This was tipped into a cheese cloth, a piece of butter muslin, and hung up over a basin in the milk house or dairy until all the whey had dripped away. This was the crowdie stage, and delicious it was when seasoned with salt. My auntie always added caraway seeds to her crowdie and left some to dry in her milk house. I preferred that to cheese that was made in a cheese press – a stone affair with weights, which could be adjusted as the cheese shrank. The whey was given to the pigs, and they had nettles boiled for them too, I remember – considered of medicinal value today. Most householders had a pig in a sty, well away from the homestead, and we used to stroke or scratch our pig's bristly back with a twig. We didn't like the animal's pink eyes, feeling that it more or less 'took our measure', so we didn't trust it too far. However, when it became pork and ham, that was a different story.

My father cured the hams with saltpetre, salt and other seasonings, and they were left in this brine for quite a time. Then they were dripped dry and hung from the kitchen rafters covered with paper or muslin. The pig's head he halved, one piece being put in the pickle with the hams, the other my mother made into scrumptious potted head, with the flesh of three rabbits, peppercorns, mace, etc., all being thoroughly minced, having simmered for hours. The mixture was then poured while hot into bowls, and how we enjoyed it next day. Some was turned out from the containers and given to friends and relations, that being the custom in those days. Venison pickled in this way was very tasty too, if steeped in water until most of the brine was removed, and fried with bacon or fresh pork. Later on, the second half of the pig's head was also made into the same delicious concoction as the first. We loved potato soup made from the pig's trotters – and the trotters, too – wishing the pig were like a centipede, providing more than just *four* legs. During the 'season', we had a pig's pail, taken down from the lodge kitchen every morning, full of odds and ends, and I must say I liked the smell of mixed-up tea leaves, fruit and vegetable leftovers.

Father washed out the pig's bladder, dried it and blew it up, tying it with string. It made a perfect balloon for us. Real balloons we got once a year from a drapery traveller and they were treasured. We liked to stroke them and smell them, as well as fly them. The bladder had a great advantage, though. It could be subjected to harsh treatment – but not the balloons! We flew a kite too, with rings of cork along its tail.

When we stopped keeping a pig, my mother sent to Wiltshire for sides of smoked bacon and these were very tasty indeed.

Family, friends and neighbours

I've written of one aunt, but I had two on my mother's side. Aunt Barbara, whose husband was an architect, was forever on the move, at her instigation. She loved flitting and never was happier than when moving. After setting up house in Ireland, England and finally Scotland, she shackled her 'itchy feet' in Lairg. Packing her household goods – and she had really beautiful things – never daunted her; she was a truly elegant person and everyone who knew her loved to help. She never enjoyed the best of health, but that did not prevent her from living life to the full. Her husband bought a two-seater coupé when we were very young, after having had a motorcycle and sidecar for many years. They arrived at our house in state to show it off, and after they had sat down to tea my lady-aunt remarked, 'How sore my neck is – I was helping Daddy round the corners!' Her brother left her his croft when he died and she entered wholeheartedly into that life with her son, and, though new to her, crofting was in her blood. She fed the hens and reared pet lambs, one of which butted her from the rear, the basket of eggs she had just collected hurtling up into the air – a complete disaster to her dignity as well as her household economy. Needless to say, that lamb was disposed of at the next livestock sale.

My grandfather, her father, had once reared a baby hind, which he called Queenie. It followed him round like a dog and when he worked in the garden – gamekeepers tended the lodge gardens – he laid his jacket on the grass and Queenie curled up on it. She escorted him when he took the gun dogs for their daily walk and he tied her up in the byre at night alongside the cows. In the mornings when she was set free, she trotted to the kitchen window for a scone and then set off after her well-loved master. Alas, one day the under keeper was on duty with the dogs and the little hind, as was customary, went too. She never came back. The man didn't miss her until he came home; probably his thoughts were elsewhere. Though my grandfather searched everywhere, calling her by name, she was never seen again. She might well have jumped into a field of turnips and been shot for fresh meat. My Uncle James, now learning his father's profession, vowed vengeance and some years later found a baby stag, which he brought home – much against his father's wishes, for this was a different kettle of fish. A domesticated stag is never a safe animal, just as a bull is a potential danger, no matter how docile he seems. The stag and my uncle became great friends, but the latter, remembering the dear little hind, taught the animal to box. He took him into the gun room at Lairg Lodge, where they stayed caretaking during the winter months. With a box filled with oats – the little box used for measuring out a horse's ration – he allowed him a few mouthfuls and then turned his back. The stag reared up on his hind legs and lashed out at him – and this was just what my wicked uncle wanted. He was sure that if anyone came near the beast – that is, other than the family – after he had trained him, that person would face the music, as it were. Sure enough, Hamish Gunn, a crofter from a nearby hamlet, took a shortcut home past the lodge when the stag was running free. It was autumn, the night was dark and the stag gave chase. His hoofs flailed the air, the crofter cleared the high gate and swore when he got home, completely out of breath and terrified, that the Devil had attacked him. The story came at once to my grandfather's ears and, as it was now the rutting season, my uncle was ordered to take his accomplice as far away on the hill as he could possibly walk – and lose him. This he did regretfully, as he had been enjoying the – to him – fun!

His sister, my Aunt Isabella, was a ladies' maid and had travelled widely, mostly abroad. She died when I was about eight years of age, so I barely remember her except that she was beautiful and played the piano to amuse us. Once when she was home on holiday, her father and herself were alone in the house. Game was plentiful in those days and she shot a black-cock from one of the windows. She plucked it and cooked it for their dinner, forgetting to remove its inside. My grandmother was horrified when she returned, ashamed that one of her daughters should be so ignorant. She might have cooked a snipe or a woodcock so, but never a bigger bird. Incidentally, the black-cock's tail was always kept to be used, when treated, in a piper's bonnet.

Isabella must have been very close to her father, because on one occasion he took her fishing to a hill loch. They arrived home minus a catch and, when questioned, admitted that they had spent a most enjoyable day walking over the hills and through the woods, eating their 'piece' (lunch) in a sheep stall. They'd never gone fishing at all because they, like my father, who of course was no blood relation, did not relish angling. The gun or rifle was their line.

Gamekeepers always kept a diary, noting down their daily movements over the hill or arable land, as the case might be, and during the season the number and nature of the game shot was carefully recorded, making interesting reading today when many species are scarce or even extinct. On one occasion when the local farmer, Mr Gray, and my father were quartering a turnip field to oust hares, one completely eluded them and the farmer said, 'Put a silver sixpence in your gun, John. That's a witch!'

In winter time, the keepers themselves went hind-stalking, sending the venison (the most delightful meat imaginable) to either proprietor or tenant, and having a little bit for themselves too. There was no poaching, maybe an occasional beast or salmon 'for the pot', but nothing like the wholesale slaughter of today. A keeper of yesteryear, alive still today, told me that he was out poaching with a shepherd on a Shinness beat and wounded a stag. They searched everywhere for it and couldn't see it, but they saw my father coming. They just lay where they were. My father paused, not looking at them, but saying, '500 yards or so to the right!'

'That,' said the keeper who told me the story, 'finished me as a poacher and I resolved to be a keeper like your father.' That he did, and became in not too long a time head keeper on the neighbouring estate.

One friend of my father's, who often visited us, always carried a white sheet in his game bag when stalking hinds in the snow. That was the first we ever heard of what was, later, camouflage. He was a most successful stalker, of course, as when he covered himself with the sheet he could creep close to the hinds. Being female, they were much more wary than the stags, but he was a master of his craft.

My father kept two ferrets. How we hated the stoat-like creatures! They had a comfortable hutch with a fine-meshed wire front to their 'dining room' and hay-filled sleeping quarters. The hutch stood on legs and had a hinged lid. Sometimes, Normanna and I had to feed the animals with porridge and milk or rabbit livers. This was done hastily, and with the lid barely raised lest the ferrets should escape. We loathed their pink-eyed glare, and though they were kept scrupulously clean, their smell!

When my father went out after rabbits, using the ferrets and nets and his gun, we were quite pleased to help skin and paunch and 'spoil' and eat them!

My mother cooked them in various ways: stewed them,

made soup of them and fried the pieces left over after dinner for tea at night. She never stuffed them, as she removed the bottom part of the spine, assuring us stoutly that that part gave a much too strong taste to the dish. Sometimes she used them in a pie.

Once, my father met a veritable host of weasels on the march; this they did when they moved to a new territory, and it was always wise, he said, to move aside and let them pass. They must have been a fearsome sight!

Traps were set – gin traps, now illegal – to catch foxes, the enemies of game birds and young lambs too. Many a weary night did our father and his terriers spend at the dens. Once he brought home four lovely little cubs and kept them for some weeks in the cosy house he made for puppies and their mothers. We used to peep at them through the wee window – they were bright-eyed, snarling terrors! They were fed like ferrets and, when old enough, were sent to a zoo.

We enjoyed visiting Mr Campbell's farmyard called the 'Square', where Mr Micklejohn, the grieve,[40] his ploughman and cattlemen made us very welcome. Single men lived in a bothy attached to the grieve's house, where his wife catered for them and kept the place clean. After they'd had a wash and their supper, they played tunes on a 'boxie',[41] as they called it. I never liked that, nor do I like the accordion, to this day! One man knitted his own stockings – he was a shepherd on the farm, so they were long, to wear with knickerbockers.

Each ploughman had a pair of Clydesdale horses and they were kept in first-class condition with curry-combs and a

---

40. Farm manager.
41. A small button-based accordion-type instrument known as a 'squeeze box'.

dandy-brush. The harness, too, was always clean and well polished, and, when a ploughing match took place in the vicinity, the horses' manes, tails and 'dossars' (forelocks) were interwoven with brightly coloured raffia or a ribbon, while every buckle shone like silver. It was a joy, at any time, to see the freshly turned furrows, like rows of chocolate soufflé steaming wetly in the sunlight.

There was a water mill at the Square, the great wheels turned by a channel of water from a large pond. Ducks swam there, and the farmhouse cook in his enveloping white apron used to come in the evening and pick up an iron ladle literally feet long and scour the bottom of the pond for eggs.

At sheep shearing, or 'clipping' time, there was great excitement on the farm – and great activity! Hirsels[42] from different parts of Mr Campbell's property came to Shinness Farm. All the shepherds were there, with dozens of collies. My father always went to lend a hand, though gamekeepers are not, as a rule, fond of sheep.

After school, we doffed our white starched pinafores and dress, put on second-best wear and, after having had something to eat, flew over the hill to the 'clipping'. Up to the granary we went, because from the rafters there hung the huge wool bags into which the fleeces were firmly packed and trampled by one of the men. As a special treat, Normanna and I were allowed to swing on the bag when it was nearly full.

The smell of tar was everywhere, as the sheep were marked with it, according to age, and hirsel and future 'requirement'. If any careless shepherd nicked a hide, tar was applied to that too.

Wooden stairs led to the granary, and once, Tom, a

42. Flocks, or the number of sheep looked after by one shepherd.

sprightly ploughman, lost his footing and fell down the steps to find himself at Mr Campbell's feet.

'Did you hurt yourself, lad?' asked the farmer.

'No, Sir,' said Tom. 'I was coming down anyway!'

I shall never forget the sound of the bleating of hundreds of sheep and lambs as they made their way back to distant fields in the summer gloaming around ten o'clock – or sometimes later. It was like that of a great organ or maybe an orchestra – with the occasional interruption of the shepherd's shout and whistle and the barking of the dogs.

The fanks,[43] where the sheep were periodically dipped, were beside the farmhouse and we used to perch on the high surrounding walls, watching the proceedings. Once, the butler's son from the lodge joined us. He was a boastful child – always lauding the wonders of England to us, the backward Highlanders. Driven beyond endurance, Normanna said, 'Anyway, we beat you at Bannockburn.'

'You never did,' he replied quickly. 'And I'll just run home and ask my dad.'

'Go,' said Normanna magisterially – she knew her history! And needless to say, he never returned *that* day! In fact, we didn't see him for quite a while afterwards.

Farming

The smell of a nice, clean byre and of the opened-up chest or 'girnel',[44] where the horses' corn was kept, were ones I liked. Meadow hay also gave off a pleasant odour, but it was difficult to harvest. It grew without a man's aid, just naturally, by the side of the loch – airy-fairy stuff that had to be

---

43. Sheepfolds with a dipping bath.
44. A storage chest for meal.

tossed for days until it dried; much more difficult than the harvesting of clover hay grown on the farms.

A scythe was used to cut it, as the soft ground where meadow hay grew was not suitable for using a horse mower. On crofts, or farms, 'roads' were first cut round the fields with a scythe before the mowers got to work, drawn by horses. On little plots the women used sickles or 'heuks' – and these they used to cut nettles too, just as they did in Old Testament days.

Reapers were used on the farms to cut the corn and the sheaves were bound by hand – that is, until the wonderful binder came along. But still the sheaves had to be set up on end in stooks by following workers. The next process was building the dried stooks into 'ackers' or 'screws' before they were eventually carted to the farm square and made into stacks. Carts had special frames attached to their sides for 'leading' home the sheaves and when the stacking was finished, rushes, or 'rashes', as we called them, were carefully placed on top of each stack as a thatch to keep out the rain. Then ropes were criss-crossed over each finished stack to secure the thatch. A little 'toorie'[45] of straw completed the edifice.

A full stack-yard gladdened the heart of every farmer and carefully fashioned stacks were something of which to be proud. A badly made one stuck out like a sore thumb – a rebuke to the builder.

Carts had their owners' names printed on a plaque at one side, and once, in Aberdeenshire, a teacher taking a religious education lesson asked the children how Joseph knew his brethren when they came to Egypt for corn. 'Please, Miss,' said a little boy. 'They'd have their names on their carts!' A true son of the soil was he.

---

45. An ornamental top or tuft.

When corn had to be threshed, the farm workers or crofter dismantled the stacks with a dog or two at hand to deal with the rats and mice that found refuge there during cold weather.

My aunt used to catch mice by balancing a bowl on a little stick above some oatmeal spread on a biscuit tin lid. The mouse touched the stick, down fell the bowl and it was imprisoned until my aunt came with a cat. And that was that!

My uncle used a flail to thresh corn sometimes. This was made of a short, rounded stick and a longer one, rather like broom handles, joined by a leather thong. He placed the sheaf on a wooden threshing floor, raised a few inches above the cement floor of the barn, and walloped the heads of grain, the long stick whirling over his shoulder rhythmically. That was just for small quantities, but for a big threshing, a mill went from farm to farm and croft to croft, together with neighbouring helpers, and this was an easier task altogether. The corn was soon in the granary above the barn, where some straw was always kept in readiness for the needs of the owners' stock animals. Fanners[46] – shaped something like a modern army tank – were used to separate the corn from the chaff. When necessary, the threshed corn was poured in at the top, a handle turned energetically and the machinery inside poured 'clean' grain through the aperture at the bottom of the fanners and chaff through the other.

The latter was often used to fill mattresses, and Normanna and I slept together on one in Granny's home when we were at the Higher Trade School. It was perfect bliss. We each snuggled down into a hollow and were as warm as pies. A hot brick wrapped up in a piece of flannelette was our

---

46. A winnowing machine or grain sifter.

hot-water bottle and a paraffin stove, shaped like a little church, kept the room cosy in severe frost. The chaff was changed three times yearly and used as bedding in byres and stables, as was fresh chaff, and of course in the pigsty too. Straw and bracken served the purpose as well.

The corn chest, kist or girnel in the stable had a wooden measure with which to fill the box in the horses' manger with corn, and to hear the champing of their teeth was a comforting sound on a stormy night when we went into the warm, sweet-smelling building when my father made his last round. The manger always had plenty of hay and the animals were watered too.

Horses were hired for the 'season', some coming from as far away as Perth, and many a trial they proved to be for the ghillies and my father, as the dealers probably thought: 'We'll send the fiery ones to the Highlands: they'll be far enough away – so far that they won't be sent back until the season is ended!' When groomed with curry-combs and dandy brushes, some horses were quite tickly and used to wriggle their skins. Often the ploughmen on the farm or the ghillies whistled through their teeth when carrying out this part of their work.

A crofter sowed his corn from a canvas basket slung across his shoulders by means of leather bands and he walked steadily, in a straight line, up and down the furrowed field, scattering the grain to left and right. His right hand swung to the left and vice versa across his midriff. It was a peaceful sight to find a man so engaged on a mild morning, devoid of wind. After harrowing the field, a scarecrow or 'bogle' or two were erected in the shape of a man with tattered clothes to frighten away the birds from the seed. This was done in potato and turnip fields as well, hence the name 'tattie-bogle'. It saddens me today to see or hear of stubble on fire after the harvest has been secured. In my young days, cattle and sheep were driven onto these fields to graze contentedly, and poultry had their share of the fallen grain, as had 'the fowls of the air'.

In spring, the hills were ablaze with muir-burn. Shepherds lit the fires usually. They wanted young grass for their flocks. The gamekeepers were much more careful about the areas set alight; they were anxious about the damage done to their game birds and their fledglings and had to hasten to the devastation – for such it was – with birch brooms to extinguish the flames. Many a weary night my father spent doing this. Sometimes mossy parts of the hill smouldered for days and had to be diligently patrolled lest a new conflagration erupted. When a plantation of trees caught fire, that was a real catastrophe and I saw his poor face burned, his eyebrows scorched and forelocks singed when he came home one early morning.

Home life

People used everything they grew and destroyed nothing that produced any good for man or beast. There was always a goodly supply of blown timber near our home and we were ready at any time to scamper off to the woods to trail home pine and birch branches snapped off from the trees during a storm. These we cut with a crosscut saw, an enjoyable and invigorating exercise. All the pieces had to be built up tidily in our peat shed away from the elements and the scent of a birch log fire was one of the prime joys of a winter's evening. Peats were cut in spring. The heathery top of the banks being just sliced off. This done, the soft brown-black turf was exposed for the actual cutting. Someone stood at the top of the bank and spread out the wet peats thrown up by the worker below. In a matter of days, if the weather was fine, the peats could be lifted and stood on end. Then after a further period of drying in the wind and sun, they were stacked in little heaps or 'rickles' and left until they were either built into big stacks on the moss or carted home, if the owner had time to do so. Funnily enough, and really quite understandably, we did not realise that the 'black oil' on everybody's lips today caused the rainbow-hued water lying in the dug out banks. We used to wonder how petrol came there, as that was how the pools looked on gravelly roads after the passage or stopping of motor cars. Our peats were left until the shooting tenants went away, though some peats were taken home in summer and built up in the peat shed behind the house.

Old people of my grandmother's generation were wise in so many ways that are coming back into vogue today. For example, the women searched the moss at certain times of the day, perhaps before sunrise, for certain blossoms and leaves, yes, and roots from which they concocted medicines and salves. If my mother, when as a little girl she stayed on holiday with her granny, cut herself while at play, she was able to go to the barn, find a clean cobweb and wrap it round the injury to stop the bleeding. This is recommended by some doctors today, I hear.

Quinine was a medicine we had to take when feverish or suffering from colds, and how we hated it. My father used to take from the medicine chest a little glass with measurements thereon, pour in some water, add the required amount of the wretched cure and we would watch the contents cloud over in swirls as he shook it up before disgustedly we swallowed it. It was, I may say, very effective nevertheless. Liquorice, syrup of figs, glycerine, gripe water, Epsom salts, Beecham's pills, Cascan, Boracic powder, Vaseline, together with bandages and a menthol cone and cotton wool were always at hand. Friar's Balsam, which smelled delightful but was mighty sore on a cut, was there too, as was iodine.

During the winter months, before going to school, Normanna had a tablespoon of malt extract, while I had Scotts Emulsion – that was our preference.

I suffered from enlarged tonsils and had them painted with a fine-haired swan-necked brush dipped in a mixture of glycerine and tannin. It nearly sickened me, of a truth, but had to be borne, as the treatment reduced the inflammation and swelling.

Weather never kept us from school. We revelled in storms, really, pitting ourselves against gusting wind and cruel rain, but thunder and lightning terrified us. Anything bright, such as a milk pail, which we sometimes carried home from a croft for our own supply, was hidden by the roadside or hanging from the branch of a tree – until my poor father came to collect it in the evening. At home, mirrors and fenders were covered with newspaper so that they did not attract the lightning.

In winter, we sucked icicles – and got scolded – and slid on the ice with glee. An S-shaped pool near our home froze over very quickly, and Hamish, the under keeper – a dear friend of us children – used to sweep it to a simply marvellous pitch of slipperiness with the stable brush. We spent hours there until my mother blew a blast on a post horn, given her by a shooting tenant as a memento when she left, to summon us for our meals.

At Lairg, there was an ice house in the birch wood below the lodge. It was dug out of a hillock deep in the ground and in winter time ice was cut up from the surface of the frozen loch and carted to this underground cave. Then it was covered all over with sawdust until it was brought forth when needed in August, just as when it had been buried.

We dared not slide on the loch, as it had freshwater wells

that only froze over lightly, once nearly causing the death of our mother in her youth as she and her friends skated in the moonlight. She was saved by her partner, who kept hold of her until some of their companions arrived to help him pull her out of the hole. It was a night of severe frost and before she reached home her long skirts were so stiff that she had to creep sideways through the door. She wanted to slip in quietly so that she would not frighten her parents!

Messrs Coats of Paisley supplied all the pupils in our school, and other small schools, with real leather school bags. The boys had straps across their shoulders, while ours were carried by hand. On the way home, on icy roads, the girls sat on their bags at the top of a steep brae and the boys shoved us away, and we careered for, I am sure, a half mile before coming to an uphill bend in the road.

Many a day we tracked dog, cat, rabbit, hare, etc., in the snow, just for fun. Often we came upon a startled rabbit hidden cosily in a clump of rashes and away it shot, its tail bobbing up and down as it disappeared over a hillock.

Curlers enjoyed their sport on a certain safe reach of the loch on the outskirts of Lairg, and played the nights – and sometimes days – away. When a bonspiel[47] took place – curlers coming from all over the county – the Higher Grade pupils were granted a half day's holiday, as the headmaster was a keen curler. When the nights were dark, acetylene lamps were hung along the shore to light the scene; to us, it was like fairyland.

Wildlife

Wild flowers were a-plenty and we picked them on our way to school, arranging them there in jam jars. Ragged robin,

---

47. A match or contest.

irises (we used the leaves for a strap when we played 'schoolies'), bluebells – which our teacher told us were really wild hyacinths, harebells[48] being the *real* bluebell – asphodel, which we called 'star of Bethlehem' because that is what it resembles. It had a sweet perfume that we could smell among the heather bells, reeking of honey. Sundew grew in marshy spots, meadowsweet by the burns, and cuckoo spit – spawn of the frog hopper – was a white mass on every other leaf in the ditches. We 'told the time' from dandelion 'clocks' to the joy of the plants but the despair of the gardeners and crofters. We were told not to tread on puffballs lest the powder blew up in our eyes and blinded us, and we must not touch the scarlet and white spotted toadstools, as they were poisonous. Wood anemones and violets grew profusely among the trees and we loved to feel the 'spring' of pine needles under our feet. We gently touched the sticky buds of horse chestnut trees as we passed the lodge garden and marvelled at the perfect horseshoe markings on the branches; when the buds opened and the beautiful 'candles' appeared, our joy was complete.

Halcyon days they were, the days of childhood. As we trotted to school on summer mornings dragonflies flitted among the trees along the roadside, their multicoloured wings a-shimmer, larks climbed to Heaven, their songs a paean of praise. Peewits shrilled and swooped round our heads, afraid of our disturbing their young, and the heart-rending cry of the curlew, which no exiled Highlander can ever forget, sounded over the moor, redolent of sadness. Yellowhammers, thrushes, blackbirds, chaffinches, willow warblers sang in the sunshine, and louder than any were the notes of the mistle thrush, whose song filled the air with wild abandon.

---

48. The round-leaved bellflower, *Campanula rotundifolia*.

61

Corncrakes called from the fields, swallows and house martins nested in the eaves of house and steading. Snipe, black game and golden plovers with grouse calling, 'Go back! Go back!' were other birds on our home ground. Different kinds of duck, oystercatchers – sometimes called mussel pickers (a much more appropriate name in this latitude) – terns and gulls nested by the loch. We used to listen to them in the evening, as they came home from foraging in the fields, while pigeons cooed among the surrounding trees. In winter, we were quite accustomed to the bugling and honking of swans, as they stayed until the loch froze over completely.

People

Going from the ordinary to the sublime, my parents loved to listen to Madame Patti[49] as she rehearsed some of her operatic roles walking by the loch when she was a guest at the lodge. Peace, perfect peace was hers and she could revel in it. Nothing but the sounds of nature disturbed her.

The highways were kept very tidy, men being appointed to different stretches of the road ultimately joining up with one another. Stone breakers were in constant employment throughout the spring, summer and autumn, breaking 'metal', as it was called, for road foundations and repairs, and gravel to cover this up was taken from pits by the roadside. Outlets were dug to drain water from the surface of the tracks and these were always kept free from grass, weeds or any other obstruction. The stone breakers were a tough fraternity. Many came from Ireland and Glasgow, with a

49. Adelina Patti (1843–1919), one of the most highly acclaimed opera singers of the nineteenth century.

smattering of Highlanders, and when they received their pay, they repaired to the hotel at Lairg, spending it on drink. First, of course, they settled their grocery bills, and weird and wonderful were the meals they concocted over the fires in their bell tents when they returned hilarious and helpless at night. Everything was put into one pan – tins of this and that – stirred, heated up and devoured with great gusto! We were never allowed to go near them, but my father used to take pity on them after any of their binges when they were too ill to lift a hammer and dosed them with medicine.

Tinkers[50] – and they lived up to their name, making different kinds of tin-tac: buckets, skillets, etc. – were a feature of our life. They made excellent pot scrubbers from heather, too, and fashioned good clothes pegs. They always used the same camping ground, whether they were Stewarts (descended from the kings of Scotland, they said), MacPhees or MacAllisters. Townsleys came from Caithness and were in those days dirty, black-visaged cave dwellers who came round the doors barefooted in winter and were really needful of whatever could be given them in the way of food or clothes, especially for their multitude of children. They swarmed all over the place! Unfortunately, the adults drank methylated spirits and were often in trouble.

Large stones held down the canvas tents which the tinkers stretched over willow or hazel hoops and these stones were always left for the next comers. It was fine to watch the smoke drift slowly from the fires outside their tents and billow away among the birch trees, seemingly to the clouds. One old woman, a MacNeill (a super clan!) and scrupulously clean, was the matriarch of her flock, and a spinster. She laid down the law with a strong arm. Her horses were first-class

---

50. Gypsies or Travelling Folk.

beasts. She bought and sold only the best and was a great favourite with everyone. We were very pleased when she came to our house with her pack, which contained a variety of drapery to suit all tastes. Pins, needles, thimbles and hairpins were common buys, too. Her cheeks were rosy, her hair screwed back tightly in a knot low on her neck, and she always wore a snow-white apron. We enjoyed her stories, as she sat in the kitchen having tea.

Once, during the First World War, she happened to be in Inverness Station when a trainload of German prisoners-of-war pulled in. 'Let *me* get my hands on them,' she shouted, and had to be manhandled off the platform before she started a riot!

On buying a horse, the old saying was:

> *One white foot, buy him.*
> *Two white feet, try him.*
> *Three white feet, deny him.*
> *Four white feet and a white nose,*
> *take off his hide and give him to the crows.*

I wonder where that bit of wisdom originated? Certainly it was often repeated in my youth. My father bought a handsome gelding with no white feet from this old woman. Perfect he was in every way, but alas, he was conscripted for the cavalry and we wept when he went.

One tinker-woman, of the Stewart tribe, resembled an Eskimo, with narrow eyes and high cheek bones. There was a theory that people from Mongolia had trekked through Siberia, crossed land and water and landed finally in Lewis long, long ago. I've often seen Lewis folk with these types of features. She was the only woman we ever saw who smoked – and she smoked a pipe!

More home life

When Daddy sowed seeds in the garden – at the lodge or at home – he did so when the moon was waxing, as he said they grew better then, and he always soaked the peas overnight before consigning them to the ground. Aruncula 'Dusty Miller', mignonette, peony roses and thorn roses grew in the boxwood bordered plots, as did lovely sweet-scented double white lilies: I think they were 'Alba Plena', which my grandfather had taken home many, many years before from the moat at Ardvreck Castle near Lochinver.

Incidentally, we never took our way past the lodge itself when tenanted but slipped quietly through the adjoining wood on a primrose-bordered path. Wood sorrel grew there, too. Many a 'treasure' for our 'housie' we salvaged from the lodge ash pit on our homeward journeys. We often used to hold a blade of grass stretched tightly between our thumbs and whistled shrilly – a great achievement – but only at school, on our way home or at our own home.

We carved our names on rowan or beech trees and watched the letters widen over the years. We were scolded for this, so it was only done very rarely. At home we blew bubbles using caked soap, a saucer filled with water and a clay pipe a-piece. Indoors we played snap, happy families, catch the ten or draughts after our homework was done and visitors were pleased to join us in our fun. Then followed cups of cocoa with biscuits – sometimes they had sugared animals on top – and, our faces and teeth cleaned, off we climbed upstairs to bed, our way lit by a flickering candle, which gave off a nice warm waxy scent, or a little lamp with a leaded bottom which never could be upset. Then, having taken off our clothes and folded them neatly, we said our prayers and got into bed.

65

Every household had huge drums of paraffin with taps, and I well remember the thrill of being allowed to take the small spouted tin to the tap for paraffin so that the various lamps might be filled. Glasses, or funnels, as they were sometimes called, had to be cleaned and polished daily, first with newspaper and then finished off with a duster. Wicks were kept neatly trimmed or the flame was uneven and smoked. I liked the smell of paraffin and smoke.

Some lamps had frosted and flowered globes over the glasses, while others had silken shades. Some stood on tables, others had reflectors and hung on kitchen walls, well out of the way of children. We used hands and fingers to make silhouettes – ducks, swans, rabbits – against the walls in the lamplight. My father excelled at this play.

Four square lanterns were in use for outside work or for visiting before the days of torches, and the lamps inside were well secured from any blast or breath of wind. These lanterns had a ring or handle on top and could be hung up in the byre, stable or barn, laid on the ground or carried by hand. We used drip-less tapers to go from room to room and light one lamp from another. When carried, the lanterns cast shadows – sometimes quite frightening, other times quite amusing. One of the crofter women used to search for her cattle at night in the woods and we used to see her lantern bobbing up and down and back and fore among the trees.

We cycled a lot when older, and Normanna had a hissing, smelly carbide lamp because she was brave, while on my bike I had a little paraffin model. Both lamps had red and green side window spots, just like ships, we thought, passing in the night: '*Green to green, and red to red. Perfect safety, forge ahead!*' We cycled freely on icy roads and reached home far more quickly than on normal gravelly surfaces. Our cycles had string contraptions from mudguard to axle on the rear wheel to keep skirts from becoming entangled in the spokes and we learned to cycle hopping on our left feet, the right one on its proper pedal. Consequently, our left boots often needed to have the soles repaired, but my father saw to that. We had all the necessary tools – lasts, hammers, nails, studs . . . and he kept us well shod without a murmur of complaint.

Our table knives were cleaned in a rotary polishing machine, something like a churn in shape, with two slits at the top having protective brass shields, and after the necessary powder had been inserted – chocolate in colour – we turned the handle a few times and the job was done. Granny had a knife board with a moleskin cover. On it the powder was lightly strewn and elbow grease was required to achieve a clean blade. We much preferred our home method! Every day spoons, forks, door knobs, fenders and fire irons were cleaned with Brasso or Silvo. The newspapers were handy – as with lamp glasses – for the first rubbing, as they kept the black residue off the dusters. For silver cutlery, we used Goddard's Plate Powder dissolved in a very little water, making a fine paste.

When my father went to Lairg to shop – very seldom, to be sure – he bought sweets: nougat, butterscotch, jujubes, and fruit (though we didn't like tomatoes, which Mother called 'love apples' and which were a very rare commodity then), and sometimes transfers. These were dipped in water and stuck on flower pots, the brown paper covers of our school books and the backs of our hands. We got pretty gummed scraps too, ready to arrange in jotters or the like. They were glossy on quite thick paper and beautifully tinted. Some were pictures of children, others flowers, horses, animals or birds. All the boys in school collected cigarette cards – valuable today.

My father made us totums.[51] He halved empty cotton reels, pointed a little stick and pushed it through the hole. We spun them around on the table, having endless fun. He made us slings and, like David in the Bible, we could use them to good effect, though not against living creatures, while my brother had a deadly catapult before graduating to a .22 rifle.

We had dolls with china heads and long fair or black hair. Some had wax faces, which were occasionally marked with our fingernails. One sailor had stubbly red hair and he was Normanna's pet. My mother made pretty dresses and petticoats for our dolls. One had swansdown round its neck and sleeve cuffs. One was a black doll in a red and white striped outfit with gold earrings. Most were gifts. I had a furry monkey, which I loved better than any doll. I took him to bed each night, hugging him close to my body, and I must have always lain on the one side, as he was completely bald where his little form touched mine. I remember after recovering from whooping cough being allowed outdoors one morning with a shawl tied round me, carrying 'Cacum' my monkey. I must have grown considerably during my lengthy illness, as the under keeper snatched the monkey from my arms and stuck it in the 'sneck' of the barn door. He often did that, but on this occasion I reached up and, to my delight, was able to get hold of my treasure, running into the house to spread the glad news.

We read any book that came into our hands at home or lent by friends. Mother had lots of prize books she had won at school and those were read avidly when we were old enough. Her aunt used to send us *Chatterbox* or *Our Darlings*[52] at Christmas and they were treasured, having

---

51. The four-sided top spun in games of chance.
52. Children's annuals.

hundreds of pages of reading, including serial stories. Dickens, Thackeray, Kipling and Robert Service were my father's favourites. Our neighbouring shepherd's sons let us have their Buffalo Bills, Dixon Hawkes and Sexton Blakes.

Each day we got the *Daily Mail* by post from Manchester and read the 'Adventures of Teddy Tail' before anyone else saw the paper. At the weekend came the *Weekly Scotsman* and *People's Friend* from Lairg. When old enough to be trusted with a lighted candle, we read in bed for a short time – which did not impair our eyesight in the least, be it said.

Each bedroom had a washstand with ewer, basin, toothbrush holder, soap dish, water carafe with tumbler, and a towel rail beside it. A commode stood beside the bed and when we were very young the 'little lamp that never upset' was left there alight during the night, or else on the landing at the top of the stairs. Hot water was brought up in a cream-lined brown can (the same as our bath). Then, washed and our beds turned down to air, we scuttled downstairs to have our hair plaited before sitting down to breakfast – porridge followed by a boiled, poached or scrambled egg with toast, and tea to wash it down.

After breakfast, we ran off to school, while at home the beds were made, rooms slopped and generally tidied, then brushed and dusted. The dressing table had a white cover and, once, Daisy's pigeon flew in, saw itself in the swing mirror and pirouetted back and fore in admiration, Mother said, until it messed up the cover and had to be evicted.

Pipe clay was used to whiten the hearth-stone in front of the kitchen range, sometimes a 'whirly' design being executed according to the mood of the worker. Fire irons were made of steel and burnished with fine sandpaper or emery cloth, while the range was polished with black lead, softened with water or Zebo. This was used for the iron kettles, too. Brasso came on the market and did away with emery cloth, with much less effort involved. Long lace curtains hung at the windows of the 'room' – 'sitting room' today – with thick serge ones alongside. These last were pulled across the 'blinded' windows on chilly evenings in winter, usually Sundays, when the room was used. The mantelpiece was bordered by a green felt 'face' delicately embroidered in a yellow flowery pattern and had 'bobbles' hanging down, which we loved to squeeze: they were soft and cushiony.

Father smoked Warlock tobacco, which had a fine scent and came, layered, in tins with little holes, pierced in circles at each end. We made spills for him, from strips of newspaper, and they looked decidedly neat when set in a wooden holder beside his chair. In the 'room', there were bought spills, made of curled slivers of wood with a delicate sandalwood smell.

Father wore mittens when out shooting in cold weather and I quickly learned to knit them. They had no tips to the fingers, so were ideal for the purpose. He was always dressed in tweed jacket, waistcoat and knickerbockers. The buttons were of horn or bone, as were the buttons on his felt spats. He had leather spats too, with little eyelets through which he tied the laces of his boots to keep them in place. They had buckles instead of buttons. Sometime during the war, puttees came to be worn and he had those, too. I cannot understand how some keepers and shepherds today can go about their business on the hills clad in trousers. How miserable they must feel, as in wet weather they cling to the legs or wallop around them! Tweed hats with earflaps were cosy in winter, and in summer these flaps were tied together on top of the hat. A hill-man always had his head covered – in summer or winter. Leather boots were handmade in Lairg and had clusters of 'tackets'[53] in threes on the sole. Hence 'tackety boots'. They had heel plates and toe plates too, and were greased with dubbin, which gives a polish as well as a waterproof finish. Melted deer tallow or goose fat, when available, also kept out the wet.

Watches were worn on a chain across the waistcoat, nestling in a pocket. This with spying-glass and game bag complete the keeper's outfit. Smart it was, serviceable and comfortable too. On Sunday, trousered suits and shoes were the order of the day. 'Nugget' or 'Cherry Blossom' polished them (and ours).

When deaths occurred in the parish, which did not seem so often as today, though the population was greater, female relatives wore mourning for some months, while men had black bands sewn to the upper left sleeve of jacket or coat, or sometimes a black diamond of material sufficed. Widows had hats with 'falls' – most becoming – with a piece of narrow white tulle or the like bordering the brim. When the period of immediate mourning was over, purple was the next colour worn. Some fine lawn black-edged handkerchiefs, kept in sachets with lavender, were always kept to wear at this time. Notepaper was black-bordered, too.

Sunny days would see us bring out our white sand shoes (gym shoes today) and we could literally fly along the roads, whereas in winter or stormy weather we wore handmade boots and galoshes. Gaiters, too, we had, with numerous bone or horn buttons, which took quite a while to fasten with a button hook – Normanna waiting impatiently for me to finish the operation, or vice versa.

Mother wore spotted veils with her hats and they were twisted into an easily untied knot under her chin. They

---

53. Small nails or hobnails used to stud the soles of boots.

added to her beauty, I thought. Hats were of straw in summer, trimmed with ribbon or flowers or both, and in winter of felt trimmed with ostrich or osprey feathers and ribbon. On occasions Mother wore black, or black and white, feather boas and they fluffed up in the wind – a source of great amusement to us. When driving to Lairg in sunshine, she held a parasol over her face and we used to creep under it too – turn about – just for fun, for we didn't mind the heat of the sun.

Once Daisy went to church with a veil on her hat and on the return journey – Mother was not with us that day – the hotel keeper's wife greeted her, 'Good afternoon, Mrs Fraser!' to her deep chagrin. My father had pulled up to speak to the lady, who was out for a stroll. That finished Daisy's first and last 'aping', in that respect, of her mother.

Our straw hats were kept on our heads with elastic round our chins (mother's had hat pins, big and small) and sometimes we pulled it and let it snap back quickly with a ping – painfully, too. Why, I know not!

Blanket washing was a great occasion, when a fire was lit early on a breezy, sunny morning among the birch trees behind the house. Two tubs were already there from the previous evening's preparations. Mother had melted bars of soap to a jelly, which she added to the first tub of hot water boiled over the flames in a big pot.

Normanna and I tucked our frocks and petticoats inside our knickers and tramped each blanket well and truly. Then mother and her helper wrung the blanket round and round a stick, rather like the handle of a broom, kept for the purpose. When this was done, the blanket was dropped into the second tub, which contained clear water, and thoroughly rinsed. This was repeated once more when the blanket, wrung tightly, was laid in the clothes basket and the process begun again with the remainder of the pile. By nightfall, all were dry and sufficiently aired for our beds, delightfully fresh and fluffy, smelling of the sweet fresh air. All day long they'd blown and swung on the clothes ropes. Some folk laid their blankets on stone dykes or bushes to dry.

Our irons were called 'box irons' and were triangular in shape, with a little flap at the back which lifted up and through the opening you put a red-hot 'heater' – the same shape as the iron but slimmer – taken from the fire. It was lifted up, with a poker inserted into a hole at its base and a second heater was immediately dropped into the embers for a replacement. We had flat irons too, which heated on a trivet in front of the fire, but I did not like them nearly so much.

The lodge laundry was near the kennels and it had a boiler, two tubs on feet, a mangle for sheets (as we had ourselves) and a wonderful pyramid-like stove with slots round it to hold irons of different sizes – the smallest for ironing and polishing gentlemen's starched evening dress collars. Those irons were quite rounded – bevelled – and fascinated us. They were at the top of the pyramid. Two laundresses worked there all week, because between personal laundry, table and bed linen, etc., there was plenty to do. Steam flowed from door and windows, and the women came out every so often for a breath of cool fresh air!

When my father's brother, a bachelor who lived with his mother and sister, ghillied on the loch, if a man was required urgently to tend a cow or a horse (the latter my auntie would never approach) she hung a solitary white apron (always used when baking) on one of the clothes lines and the crofter who lived a little way up the hill at the back of the house – Big Alick – would hasten to her aid. Similarly, if she made a clootie dumpling[54] during the university vacations, she displayed a black apron, so that the policeman's son, a budding doctor, knew what we were to have for supper and he joined the feast. No telephone was speedier.

We had much happiness at Christmas time, but did not fuss about New Year. Holly was difficult to get, so my father used to bury rowan berries – we had plenty – in a sealed biscuit tin box in the garden and just before Christmas he dug it up and intertwined the berries with ivy, making a pretty, colourful decoration for our rooms. Once, he forgot just where he had buried the tin and had to dig up the whole of the plot. No one had his plot dug at that time of the year but him, poor dear! We always had roast pork (cold) for breakfast on Christmas and New Year mornings and at dinner time, around one o'clock, soup, stuffed fowl, vegetables, plum pudding, jelly and custards. The jelly cooled in a Delft mould shaped like a strawberry and was most attractive when turned out. The farm grieve and his wife came to dinner with us on Christmas Day. On Christmas Eve, our black woollen stockings were tied together with safety pins over the brass rail at the foot of the bed and in the morning we woke to the interesting 'bulges' before our gaze and to the tantalising smell of tangerines and apples, which, with our other little things, had been slipped into our stockings. Then there were parcels for each of us lying at the bottom of the bed. Hurriedly we opened our 'surprises' by the light of a candle. I'll never forget the year Normanna got ludo and we tried to eat the little counters – so like sweets. I got a game like Meccano but consisting of different sizes of tin tubes to make into so many shapes, so many constructions. That year, of course, as always, we set out to

54. A dumpling wrapped in a cloth and boiled.

show our parents the presents that we had from Santa, but at the top of the stairs just outside our bedroom door I over-balanced with my load and off I sailed, scattering the treasure trove noisily in every direction. It would *have* to be me – and the whole household sprang out of bed at the commotion. Mother used to call us 'chick-a-biddies', but not that morning!

Mrs Campbell and Mrs Gray, another farmer's wife, used to invite us turn about to a party at this time of year and it really *was* a party. We didn't have a Christmas tree at home, but there was always one at Mrs Campbell's, with a lovely gift for each child. At Mrs Gray's, there was a bran-tub also with gifts. We had a 'set' tea, with sandwiches and all kinds of cakes, and then played merry games, the older folk joining in the merriment. The Grays' farm was about five miles distant, so Father conveyed us there in the trap. On a moonlit night as we came home, we used to lie back in our seats, watching the trees glide by while the horses' shoes struck sparks from the frosty road and the stars twinkled down at us from the clear blue sky. It was magic! We looked up at the man in the moon and, in our innocence, thought he was enjoying himself too.

In the autumn, a traveller came from Glasgow and Mother ordered quantities of groceries for her winter store. He cycled from parish to parish, his pockets bulging with valuable jewellery – no muggers then! – as well as a thick notebook in which he entered one's orders. There was great excitement when the goods arrived in wooden boxes: tins of Mazawattee Tea, with Indian women in saris pictured in tea gardens, treacle, syrup, sugar, marmalade . . . and always some presents for the household as discount.

It was an adventure going over the moor where lived a dressmaker who sometimes made clothes for special occasions. She went round us on her knees, adjusting hems with pins in her mouth, and we were terrified lest she swallow them.

On our way, the wind whistled through spaces in the dykes – no cement was used in the dykeing craft, little stones being inserted instead among the larger ones. The walls made a shelter for the animals instead of the fences of today, with their cruel strands of barbed wire! There were 'stalls' – sheepfolds – here and there on the moors to shelter sheep. They were built like the dykes but circular in shape, instead of long lines enclosing a field. The stalls had a gate so that the shepherd could shut in a goodly number of his flock, should he wish, but usually the aperture was left open and the ewes and lambs could huddle inside away from the wind coming from any direction. How wise were the old-time farmers and shepherds; even outside the stalls there was shelter from the storms. As far as gates were concerned, crofters were notorious for having very few real ones! Bed ends, poles slipped through iron rings in the dykes, crossbars – anything that would keep an animal where it should be, but rarely a good substantial gate. Of course, money was scarce, so probably that was the reason why our farms were furnished in that way.

Going to school or coming home in hot weather, we often found ewes on their backs, unable to rise because of the weight of their fleeces, so we went in a body to help them up. The shepherd who lived near us told us to hold on to them until they got their bearings, as they might well blunder along with us instead of running away. When we found a little dead lamb, we buried it under a cairn of stones and the shepherd's youngest son used to go down on his knees and offer up a prayer. We solemnly stood by, convinced that one day he would probably become the minister of the church.

He might have done so had today's grants been available then, but for one member of a big family in wartime that was out of the question. He became a shepherd – a good one, too – in later life – and what better profession, for did not our Lord call himself the Good Shepherd?

In a corner of a sheltered field stood a little hut with a small yard in front. It was called the 'keb'[55] house and here at lambing time were penned recalcitrant ewes who would not accept their lambs or who had lost their lambs and were given a pair of twins belonging to another ewe. The dead lamb's skin was pulled over the foster child's body and it was quickly accepted by the new mother. After some weeks we would see these lambs with their overcoats sadly in tatters, but seemingly quite happy.

Another trick was to put paraffin on the ewe's nose and on the strange lamb, which usually worked. Someone told me lately that he'd seen hairspray do exactly the same. A sweeter perfume, no doubt, but what would the shepherds of my day have said to that?

We often plaited rushes on our way home from school and gathered wool cast off by the sheep, comparing it with the pure white bog cotton. One year, Normanna and I collected sufficient wool near our house with which to have a travelling rug made at the east coast wool mill in Brora. How proud we were of that achievement! We had to be careful, keeping to the sheep tracks that wound this way and that because of adders. My father once killed one for us to take to school, putting it in a glass jar into which the science teacher poured spirit. So far as I know it is preserved there in all its evil elegance to this day.

Many were the superstitions believed in by most people.

---

55. A small shed or shelter.

After all, there was no radio or television, so old beliefs were passed on in stories from generation to generation. A dog howling in the night-time was an ill omen – maybe news of an approaching death, as was a cock crowing in the hours of darkness.

'*Blessed is the bride that the sun shines on, and the coffin on which falls the rain*'; '*cut your nails on Sunday, your safety seek. The Devil will have you the rest of the week*' – these were commonplace sayings. An itchy left hand meant a gift was coming your way, while an itchy right hand denoted the advent of a visitor. Sneezing – '*One a wish, two a kiss, three a disappointment, four a letter, five something better, six a journey you'll go*'. 'See a pin and let it lie – you're sure to want before you die. See a pin and pick it up, all the day you'll have good luck.' A wise one that. For a bride – '*Something old, something new, something borrowed, something blue*' – still a universal saying.

If you should chance to break something, like a plate or cup, go and break two matches or the like, for you shall surely otherwise complete the hat-trick of breakages. This I have proved myself on many occasions. Break a mirror – seven years bad luck. '*Don't cast a cloot [any kind of clothes or cloth] till May [hawthorn] is oot!*'

These and many more we knew from childhood. When I read about the power of the African witch doctor, I was not at all surprised because there is something primitive in us all, though we are Christians, when such beliefs survive today. Perhaps I should say 'survive among my age and generation' – the young have their own new world and the 'man in the moon' is no more.

My memories are principally of fun and happy people – hard-working, but finding pleasure in executing their daily tasks, and who had time to glory in the beauty of the world around them: the moors, woods, hills, lochs, birds and beasts; to whom little children were God's greatest gift, whether their own or another's, it mattered not.

In plucking the fruit of memory, one runs the risk of spoiling its bloom – so said Joseph Conrad. I sincerely hope I have *not* done that.

Ann Gray, of Colaboll, Lairg

———— ◆ ————

Ann Gray was born at Colaboll Farm on 24 May 1906, the youngest of five children born to John Gray and his wife Mary McInnes. The eldest was Margaret, affectionately known in later life as Meg, followed by three brothers, Angus Francis (Frank), John Malcolm and Alexander. The family suffered a severe blow in November 1916 when Frank, who was serving with the 5th Battalion Seaforth Highlanders, was killed in action at Beaumont Hamel in the Somme.

Ann's father John was one of the Grays of Culmaily, Lairg, who had gone into partnership with Daniel Murray of Drumnahaving, Lairg, taking on the tenancy of Achinduich Farm, as well as establishing the Mail Contracting and Carting business of Gray & Murray, forerunner to the Sutherland Transport & Trading Company. When the lease of Achinduich Farm expired, John and Daniel acquired a 19-year tenancy of Colaboll Farm from Whitsun 1885, the lease having been relinquished by Walter Stuart, Master of Blantyre. Iby Fraser notes that John Gray was a keen 'Volunteer', taking part in rifle competitions. In 1897, Gray took over from J.R. Campbell as 'lieutenant' of the Volunteers, following a petition from the private soldiers requesting him to do so. On several occasions he was a competitor at the national shoots, first at Wimbledon and later at Bisley, from where he brought home many awards.

In 1911, when Ann started school, her brother Alex was already attending Lairg Higher Grade School, as it was then, so it was there she attended rather than Shinness School.

Charles Gray – the grandson of Alexander Gray, John Gray's brother – recalls being told how John would take them to Lairg with a horse and cart. Ann spent ten years in Lairg School, until June 1921; thereafter she followed in the footsteps of her brother Alex by attending Dingwall Academy for two years to sit her Lower and Higher exams. English, Latin and French were passed at Higher level and Maths at Lower level, giving her the requirements for going to university.

Ann commenced studies towards an MA degree at Edinburgh University on 23 October 1923 in the company of her school friend Iby Fraser, who also grew up in Shinness, being the daughter of the gamekeeper on Shinness Estate. In her first year in Edinburgh, Ann lodged at 18 Warrender Park Terrace with her recently married first cousin, James MacKay, and his wife Janet, whose son James Peter MacKay became Lord Chancellor in 1979, as Lord MacKay of Clashfern.

Due to his father's illness, Alex had to give up his plans to be a vet and left his studies to return home to help his father and eventually take over the running of the farm when John Gray died in March 1924 in his 76th year.

During the course of her three years at Edinburgh University, Ann studied English, Latin, French, Moral Philosophy and History of Art. Her exam results demonstrate that French was not her strongest subject; she had to re-sit it in order to graduate, in contrast with all her other subjects, which she passed at the first attempt.

Ann graduated in September 1926, having passed her French re-sit with flying colours, and commenced her teacher training at Moray House in October 1926. Following the completion of her teacher training in June 1927, Ann was appointed to her first teaching post, at Invergordon Academy, commencing in August 1927 on a salary scale of £180 to £300 per annum. There followed 22 years of service in Invergordon, including the duration of the Second World War.

The writers of Ann's obituary, published in the *Northern Times* in September 1997, recalled:

During the war she was a member of the VAD (Voluntary Air Defences) team and was trained by the Red Cross in anti-gas procedures, and also to drive a truck and ambulance.

When the senior classes at the Academy were sent to Dingwall for safety reasons, she was left behind with the remainder, to hold the fort, so to speak, and with instructions to run for the trenches whenever the siren sounded – these having been dug in the back yards of the houses on the high street.

There were a number of false alarms, when the pupils spent their time crouched in the trenches, singing popular songs until the all-clear was given. On one particular day when the oil tank at the harbour was hit by the Germans, she had been walking between the school buildings. Fortunately no one was hurt.

In 1949, Ann took up a post in Lairg Higher Grade School, as teacher of English and Latin, and returned to stay with Meg and Alex in the family home at Colaboll.

Ann spent the next 20 years in Lairg School as a highly regarded teacher and disciplinarian, greatly esteemed by all her pupils. Her sole regret was the witnessing of the school being downgraded, first to a junior secondary school, then to a non-language school in 1961, and finally to a primary-only school.

In her school, university and early teaching days, Ann was an enthusiastic sportswoman. She was one of the original members of the Lairg cycling club. At Dingwall Academy, she excelled at hockey as a member of the girls' team and loved to play tennis. She was even game for a round of golf – Roger Watt, the great-great-grandson of Ann's aunt, Annie McInnes, remembers Ann telling him her story of once being told by a professional, 'Your problem is that you're standing too close to the ball after you've hit it.' In later years, Ann loved nothing better than to travel, both locally and afar. Cousins visiting from Australia were treated to grand tours of Sutherland by car and she was very mindful of visiting relations such as the Watts in Harpenden, as well her niece, Gilda, and nephew, Peter, both in London.

Ann played a very full role in the community and in her beloved Lairg Free Church, of which she remained a faithful member all her life, following in the footsteps of her parents. She had a great knack of knowing the right word for the right moment and was always willing to give encouragement to others. She possessed a wonderful memory for texts and passages from the Bible and loved psalm singing, having a grand alto voice. Her Christian standing in the community was exemplary and she was highly respected both within and outwith the church.

Amongst Ann's many community interests were the debating society, WRVS, Guiding and the Red Cross. Along with brother Alex she was a strong supporter of, and participant in, the Lairg Crofter's Show. She was regularly called upon to be a judge in the industrial tent. Growing indoor bulbs every winter gave her great pleasure and she enjoyed exhibiting them at SWRI meetings in the village.

When the Lairg History Society was formed in 1993, she went along to some of the earlier meetings to share her knowledge of life in Lairg when she was growing up in Colaboll. Being interested in history, she wrote a piece entitled 'History of the Lairg Free Church' and an account of Colaboll Farm steading, which had suffered a devastating fire when she was young.

Colaboll had always been a very welcoming place. Meg was always a very warm-hearted hostess and a great cook, having learned both at her mother's side and during her time in the Land Army throughout the First World War. Sadly Meg died soon after Ann retired in 1969, but although never as domesticated as Meg, Ann ably carried on the tradition of hospitality. She had learned as a youngster to welcome all and sundry to the farm, including tramps and travelling people, the 'Summer Walkers' who once roamed the roads of the north. The barns of Colaboll Farm provided a welcome haven for them to sleep for the night.

When her brother Alex took ill in the mid-1970s, Ann dutifully and caringly looked after him until a few days before his death in 1979, aged 79, having been born on 12 January 1900, 'Old New Year's Day'.

Ann's retirement stretched for twenty-eight years and, apart from the last two, when she was in Oversteps Home in Dornoch, she lived on her own in the old cottage at Colaboll and continued to be actively involved in many pursuits in the community. She celebrated her 90th birthday while residing in Oversteps.

Ann died in the Cambusavie Unit in Golspie on 18 August 1997 aged 91. She was the last remaining member of her generation of the family but is survived by her brother Malcolm's daughter and son, both of whom are married with family and live near London.

Changed Days in the Colaboll Steading

———— ✦ ————

I have been thinking of all the changes in the Colaboll Steading over the last 100 years.

My father came to farm here in 1885 – not so very long after the land in Shinness had been reclaimed. There were four farm cottages (two double houses) built by 1874, but there was no farmhouse until 1892. The first tenant, the Master of Blantyre, farmed Colaboll along with his Scibercross Farm, which he made his headquarters. However, there was at Colaboll a very big steading, with stables, byres, two large folds, a large barn and, above, a fine big granary, with two smaller ones leading off it. The main granary was wood-lined and had big rafters holding up the roof. When wool was being packed, the long wool-bags were slung up by strong ropes and the ropes left for a few days when the bags were removed. It was my delight to make a swing with them and try to swing from one rafter to the next. There were in the granary a winnowing machine, an oilcake crushing machine, a brass-bound bushel measure for grain with a kind of rolling pin for levelling off the grain at the top, and a weighing machine for sacks of grain. In a smaller granary, there was a compartment called a 'girnel', where bolls of oatmeal were stored. I imagine the oats were milled in the Gruids

Mill – the ruins of the mill can still be seen. Then there was a barrel of treacle somewhere else. If you removed the spigot, you could get a lick of the treacle on the q.t.

In the big barn, there was a threshing machine – in the early days, I believe, it was quite usual to have 70 to 80 corn stacks in the yard behind the steading. I think this mill was driven by one of the steam engines left over from the reclamations. It was fired by peat and was in the charge of Donald Ross, who lived in the Luncheon House and whose duty it had been to attend the Duke of Sutherland when he came there on his way to visit the work of reclamation. The duke came by launch up Loch Shin to a point below the Luncheon House and was met by a carriage and pair driven by David Ross, who took him on to the works and who afterwards was cattleman at Coloboll for nearly 40 years.

Later an oil-engine was installed, and later still, because the barn was large, elevators were installed as well, to carry the straw to whatever point it was required. There was a series of sliding doors that could be opened to let the straw drop at the right spot. It was no longer necessary to fork the straw into position.

There were cows with calves, and usually about five milking cows in the byres because there were five families to supply with milk. These cows were milked by two girls, who also helped in the house. There was butter and crowdie to be made, and cheese too – I remember an old iron cheese press that stood near the back door, but it was no longer in use in my time.

In the stables, there were Clydesdales, three pairs, and one or two lighter ponies, as well as foals and colts. There were regular visits by a groom in charge of a Clydesdale stallion. The colts used to be called in on a winter evening by someone going out and calling, 'Cope, cope, cope'. That brought them in to be fed and watered. What the origin of the word 'cope'[56] is, I don't know.

Pigs, too, were housed in the steading and quite large litters were often produced. A fattened pig might be killed and each household got a share. This also happened when a sheep was killed. There followed much business in the kitchen, making black puddings and white puddings and preparing tripe.

I have vague memories of a big ploughing match held in one of the fields now covered by Loch Shin. It must have been about 1913. The horses taking part had been groomed to perfection, their harness and brasses polished till they shone, while manes and tails were dressed with brightly coloured ribbons. There were prizes for the best-looking horses, as well as for the straightest furrows.

The Great War brought many changes. Two men were immediately called up because they had joined the Territorial Army. One of these was my oldest brother, Frank. He had been studying at Aberdeen University, but he was killed at Beaumont Hamel in 1916. The other was the cattleman's son, who survived the war.

During the war years, two or three men from the Labour Corps came to help at busy times, for example harvest time. They bothied in the Luncheon House. Most of them had seen active service. One who stayed on after the war had lost an eye.

My second brother, Malcolm, was at Aberdeen Grammar School when war broke out, but he later joined the RNAS [Royal Naval Air Service] and served on HMS *Campania*,

---

56. Or 'cop', a contraction of 'come up'.

which was the first ship to have a deck from which aircraft could take off. The RNAS was subsequently amalgamated with the RFC [Royal Flying Corps] to form the RAF.

My youngest brother, Alex, was at Dingwall Academy at this time but left to help on the farm, my father being about 70 then. My only sister, Meg, spent the war years training girls for farm work, first in Kent and later in West Malvern.

I have read that the autumn of 1914 was a particularly fine one. This reminded me of the old laborious methods of harvesting of long ago.

In early days, the crop was cut by a mower, which meant that sheaves had to be made by hand. First a band to bind the sheaf was made by joining together two sets of stalks very firmly, to stand rough handling and forking. The knack had to be thoroughly learned. The sheaves were stooked (set up) in the correct position to take advantage of the prevailing wind as much as possible. When stooks were dry enough for stacking, the 'leading' began – in other words, carting the sheaves to the stackyard. Carts were fitted with frames on which a big square load could be built. Making a good load was a special skill, as, even more so, was the building of a stack that would withstand winter weather. The cutting machine, known as a 'binder', was quite a big advance on the mower, since it made and bound with twine the sheaves, which it then threw out. Today the combine harvester can cope with harvesting and threshing in the one operation.

In the early '20s, my father became ill and he died in 1924. From then on, my brother was in full charge, assisted by my sister. He was particularly interested in his horses and liked nothing better than breaking in young animals.

Unfortunately, in 1929 there was a disastrous fire in the steading and, since it happened in February, the steading was full of animals. It broke out in the engine room during a threshing session.

My brother had taken my mother to visit her sister in Culmaily but, seeing the smoke from a great distance, came home in double-quick time. There were, of course, no telephones and no fire engines.

The first priority was to save the animals. This the men on the spot, along with helpful neighbours, did most nobly. Only a few pigs, and a cow that followed its calf when it turned back into the blazing building, were lost. But gone was the great slated roof, except that covering one of the small granaries; gone, too, were the barn, the long wood-lined granary and the threshing mill.

As it was February, to stable horses and house cattle was a major problem. Three pedigree mares that had been kept for breeding were sold. The horses were stabled in the cart shed and the implements shed, which were still usable, and some cattle were kept in the folds. Neighbours also helped to solve the problem until warmer weather came.

Rebuilding began in May, and by October everything was ready to cope with the harvest, a new engine and a thresh-ing-mill having been installed. The whole building was considerably smaller but, in some respects, more convenient.

The barn at Colaboll had sheltered many a vagrant over the years, and in the '20s and '30s after the Great War scarcely a week passed without one or two men spending a night there. These men were not the regular tramps, who might appear once or twice a year. They were ex-servicemen, looking for work. I remember one of them selling copies of rather pathetic poems of his own composition. The refrain of one of them was 'No more war'.

I can remember the names of several regular tramps. There was Jimmy Paterson, who carried a bag of books on his back. He was said to have been a law student but, having been jilted, he took to the road. Not willing to give up his matches, he slept in the open cart shed, where he read his books by the light of a candle. There was 'Big Fraser'. He had been a stone-breaker in the days before tarmac. On his last visit after coming out of Peterhead Prison Hospital, he said he would like to die on the top of Ben Loyal. There was the 'Irish Fiddler', who thought there was no place like Ireland, although he seemed to keep his distance from it. He was a sad man on his last visits. Someone had stolen his fiddle. There was John Street, who was apt to shout out at the pitch of his voice from time to time as he walked along. There was 'Happy Harry'. On occasion he helped at the potato-lifting, but it was said that he ate more than he lifted. There was 'Galloway', who sold bits and pieces from a basket. He felt the local merchants didn't like to see him coming into the area. 'Darkle' Smith did a bit of selling, too. He wanted meths for rubbing on his leg (?). There was 'On Tour', a cheery fellow with a sense of humour. He wore a placard saying 'On Tour' but complained of having difficulty with his balance of payments. There was Ivan Glover, a simple soul who admitted to being a bit simple: 'But then,' he said, 'everybody's a bit simple. Some know it, the others don't.' So, who was the wise one?

I think the last to frequent the barn in the '70s was a Welshman, Morgan Morgan. He once had eardrops he got from a doctor. I was called in to do first aid. This I duly did and I got a letter of thanks later, with a poem he had written, telling of some of his experiences on the road. One cattleman kept what he called his 'Visitors' Book' and several of these names appeared in it.

The '30s were the difficult years after the Great Depression and agriculture suffered like every other industry. By that time, tractors were in use and the need for horses grew less.

In the winter months, the steading was always full of animals that had to be fed, watered and mucked out. There was plenty of activity, but in summer there were only occasional busy periods – perhaps threshing sessions, sheep shearing or, especially in August and September, preparation of lambs and ewes for the Lairg Sale.

Until the late 1940s, sheep from the north and west were 'walked' to the Lairg Sale. That usually meant about a week on the road for sheep, shepherds and their dogs, from as far away as Durness and Kinlochbervie. They made their last stop before proceeding to the Mart at Colaboll so that for one night there were hundreds of sheep on the fields. Shepherds and dogs had to be fed and housed for the short period of rest they might get during the hours of darkness; I've seen more than a dozen dogs being fed, for every shepherd had two dogs.

Then, very early on sale morning, there would be much whistling and shouting as the various flocks got on the road for the last five miles to Lairg Station, where the sale was held. Nowadays, of course, double-decker floats carry the sheep and the long laborious trek is no longer necessary.

In the '30s, there were some interesting camps held on the farm. On one occasion the County Guide Camp was held in one of the big fields. During three or four consecutive years, Captain Ronald Wills, of the tobacco firm, brought 20 to 30 boys from a boys' club in Bath to camp on the banks of Loch Shin. It was the usual practice to give them breakfast in the farmhouse on the morning of their departure. Thus they were able to pack up all their gear and cooking utensils the night before.

Later, during the war years, there was a Forestry Camp for

men and women employed in cutting down several of the woods on the Shinness Estate. During these years, too, there were sheepdog trials held in aid of 'Wings for Victory' or one of the other wartime funds.

During the Second World War, an Indian Mule Company was stationed for a time in Lairg after the withdrawal from Dunkirk. Sheep for the Muslim diet were supplied from the farm. These sheep were slaughtered at the local slaughterhouse in a method that horrified the local butcher. A small vacant church was used as a mosque and the muezzin came out to the steps to call the faithful to prayer at the set times. The building, which is now the Lairg Dairy, was the Indians' sick bay. One day, the orderlies there were surprised to find themselves on the carpet before their British Officers, who lived with their wives not far away. The charge was wolf-whistling after the wives of the officers as they passed by. It transpired that the guilty party was the parrot who lived next door!

Over the years, there have been one or two rather unusual men working with us. In the '30s, there was Luke Welsh, who arrived looking for work. He was quite content to have a bed in the stable loft, while he was fed in the kitchen. He did all sorts of odd jobs, including scullery work and gardening. He hailed from Lancashire, where he had been a miner. From there, he went to the Fort William area, but he had a drink problem which put an end to his work there. However, he didn't blot his copybook overmuch while he was at Colaboll.

One day when he was peeling potatoes, I asked, 'What kind of potatoes are these, Luke?'

'Well,' he replied, 'I don't rightly know, Miss Ann, but I think they are Glories of 'Eaven.' Later I discovered they were Beauties of Hebron.

I remember that he went back to Darwen for a holiday and, to our surprise, he brought little gifts to various people.

Another man, also an Englishman, but he came from the south coast and was a very different type. I think his Christian name was Harold, but everyone called him 'Mr Kidd'. He and a friend had been colporteurs[57] in Abyssinia when the Great War had broken out. Later they tended a Highland soldier who, when he was dying, asked them to write to his mother. They did better than that. After the war, they came north to visit the relatives at Kinlochbervie. His friend returned south, but Mr Kidd remained in the north. In due course, he came to live in a cottage in West Shinness, but later moved to a little wooden house in Lairg. From there, he used to come to work in Colaboll. He had a bicycle on which there was a large carrier for books, which he sometimes distributed as in his colporteur days. This was irreverently called the 'Bible Hurley'. For us, he worked in house and garden, but his great interest was the poultry, especially the ducks, which would set up a great quacking as he approached in the morning. He was a kindly Christian who lent a hand to many people in the district.

A third man we knew as 'McBride'. He had had a somewhat chequered career. After working in the tunnel for the hydro-electric scheme at Pitlochry, he came to this district to work on a drainage scheme. Later he became handyman and gardener to the local doctor. Finally he worked for some time at Colaboll.

He would turn his hand to any job on the farm, but he also had unusual gifts. He wrote several serious poems of merit and he could produce clever crayon sketches. Unfortunately, a chest complaint contracted in the Pitlochry

---

57. Distributors of books and religious tracts.

tunnel forced him into hospital for some time. He recovered sufficiently to occupy a bungalow in Inverness, where he lived comfortably until his death in the '70s. He was a remarkable man, but he had an even more remarkable son. Here is an extract taken from a newspaper article written when that son visited him in Inverness:

Mr Duncan Pryde answered an advertisement for an Alaskan fur trapper and emigrated when he was 18. He spent 18 years working with the Eskimos, and learned their language. He joined the Hudson Bay Company and after three years trading with Indians in the Canadian Tundra, he moved to the North West Territories to establish posts for Eskimo tribes – living in a snow house, travelling by dog-sled and sharing the language and customs. His latest achievement is the title of 'professor' – without as much as an 'O' Grade to his name. He has a staff of 30 at the world's first Eskimo University, at Barrow, Alaska. Now he is on an all-expenses-paid trip to Paris, Copenhagen, Washington and Greenland as part of a study programme.

Duncan Pryde told the story of ten years of Eskimo life in a book entitled *Nunaga*, published in 1972.[58]

In the '50s, great changes came, not to the steading but to the farm. These were brought about by the Shin Hydro-Electric Scheme. The level of the loch was raised to such an extent that nearly half of the farm went under the water. Much of the land was out-run, but some of the best fields disappeared too. So too did the smithy and the smithy house that had been run in connection with the farm, as well as fine trees that had to be cut down. The road to

---

58. Currently published by Eland Books, ISBN 0907871631.

Lairg was realigned, which meant that we were now four miles from Lairg by road instead of three. It was found for some time after the waters covered so much new land that the fishing was particularly good. One man telling me of the fine trout he had caught said, 'I caught it in one of your fields!'

A smaller farm meant a change in policy. Cropping was reduced and there was greater emphasis on cattle and sheep. A cattleman, a tractor man and one other man, with casual labour, were now usually sufficient.

In spite of Hydro Board assurances to the contrary, the lower double house proved to be too near the water. A big storm brought the loch up to the doorstep. Consequently, it had to be abandoned and a new semi-detached building for two families was erected beside the other double house, which now provided housing for different families needing accommodation on a temporary basis. That was the position until the '70s.

By that time, I had given up my teaching job and was able to look after my sister, who became ill in 1969. She died in 1970 and by that stage I had learned to housekeep, cook, bake and even to make butter and crowdie.

In 1975, my brother decided to retire from the farm and a generous laird allowed us to occupy the modernised double house, now a very comfortable single one. The flitting after 90 years' occupation was quite an undertaking, but after all it was only from one side of the steading to the other.

The new tenant was a young farmer naturally intent on changing to more modern methods. He concentrated on silage making and stock farming. The steading was altered to provide a large cattle court. When Dalchork was added to the Shinness Estate, it was farmed along with Colaboll.

In the '80s, new tenants took over. They now farm Dalchork, with their farm at Balblair. After a year or so, all the cattle were sold off. Two very large slatted wooden sheds – one at the front and one at the back – were added to the steading. These were for goats!

In October 1987, 800 goats arrived from New Zealand.